marie claire
luscious

Acknowledgements

A heartfelt thanks to Kay Scarlett and Juliet Rogers for allowing me once again to get lost in the world of food and for allowing me my desert island escape. Thanks also to Jackie Frank for giving me the opportunity to work on the marie claire titles.

A huge thank you to Marylouise Brammer for sacrificing many a weekend in the pursuit of a beautiful design and book. Thank you for your time and endless enthusiasm. A big hug goes to Zoë Harpham for her patience in organizing not only this book but also its author, and for her bravery in the face of a scary deadline. What seemed like a rocky climb turned into a gentle stroll along the beach. A very big thank you once again.

Jo Glynn, as always, did a wonderful job testing the recipes and keeping me on track and Katri Hilden kept a sharp editorial eye on my words and wording. Indeed, a big thank you to the whole team at Murdoch Books.

A cookery book has to make you hungry when you look at it and once again Ross Dobson has been the saint in the kitchen. His cooking has turned a recipe into a gorgeous tumble of ingredients and for that he deserves several big hugs and probably a few stiff drinks. Mikkel Vang and Christine Rudolph took the food, added a spoonful of beautiful light, a sprinkle of gorgeous props and a dollop of island magic and created the luscious images that tell this book's story. A big hug for both of you and a very big thank you for all your hard work.

Books have a habit of taking over your life. As always, the biggest thank you goes to Warwick who has provided love, laughter, critical tastebuds, and that all important commodity, time. Thank you also to Ben and Sam for forgiving me my occasional absent-minded mothering and for filling the fridge with food you weren't interested in. Apparently not everyone is as excited by chilli prawns and duck salad as I am!

marie claire
luscious
simply delicious food

michele cranston

whitecap

contents

simple fresh food

This new cookbook series is all about introducing a sense of place while still remaining true to the idea that food should be easy, great tasting and healthy. With this in mind, I thought it might be nice for this book to indulge in a little escapism. While I admit that this was somewhat of a selfish desire on my behalf to run away from the daily madness of a busy life filled with children and work, I suspect that I am not the only one who daydreams about sitting under a swaying palm tree.

I don't know what it is about sandy beaches and blue seas but when most of us think of escaping there's often a desert island thrown into the plan somewhere along the way. Is it the mesmerizing heat, the perfect emptiness of a watery horizon or just that calming sense of being away? Whatever the attraction, when we think of indulgent relaxation we tend to think of locations such as these. And when I start to think of such places my mind turns to food … of course!

8

Luscious tropical fruit, leafy bowls of salad, grilled seafood, tangy Asian noodles and spiced couscous … food that not only tastes great but is good for you. Food that is bursting with colour, dripping with yummy juices and spiced with a splash of lime, a scattering of herbs and a sprinkle of seasoning. While most of us can't sit in a crystal sea eating juicy ripe mangoes with salty hands we can sit down to a beautiful salad of fresh papaya and briny prosciutto. And that is the wonderful thing about food — that it can, in a simple mouthful, take us to another place.

So let's all lose ourselves on an idyllic island somewhere in the middle of a perfect sea … even if only for an hour or two. And don't panic about the task ahead — while I may have become lost in the thrall of ingredients and flavours, I've kept my feet planted firmly in the sand. The recipes are easy and use simple ingredients, so you too can relax and enjoy the journey.

fruit

sunny days   tantalizing flavours

tangy bite sweetness and light

The first chapter is fruit … well it had to be really as nothing implies sunshine and healthy eating more than a big bowl of ripe and luscious fruit. It's a great way to start the day, to offset the richness of succulent meats like pork and duck or to delight the tastebuds at the end of a meal — whether it's high-summer peaches with their blushing sunset skins, the tropical lushness of large, rainbow-hued mangoes or simply a pile of perfect jewel-toned berries. Just sit back and enjoy, knowing mother nature has already done the hard work for you …

nutty banana bread

90 g (3¼ oz) butter
2 eggs
175 g (6 oz/½ cup) golden syrup or honey
250 g (9 oz/2 cups) plain (all-purpose) flour
2 teaspoons baking powder
½ teaspoon bicarbonate of soda (baking soda)
2 large ripe bananas
100 g (3½ oz/1 cup) pecans, roughly chopped
2 tablespoons poppy seeds
1 tablespoon grated lemon zest
butter, extra, to serve
sliced mango, to serve
plain or Greek-style yoghurt, to serve

Preheat the oven to 180°C (350°F/Gas 4). Lightly
grease an 8 x 22 cm (3¼ x 8½ inch) loaf (bar) tin
and line it with baking paper.

Put the butter, eggs, golden syrup, flour, baking
powder, bicarbonate of soda and bananas in a food
processor and blend to a smooth dough. Add the
pecans, poppy seeds and lemon zest and pulse
until just combined.

Pour the mixture into the loaf tin and bake for
40 minutes, or until a skewer inserted into the centre
of the loaf comes away clean. Allow to cool in the tin
before slicing. Serve warm, generously spread with
butter, or toasted with sliced mango and a dollop of
yoghurt. Makes 10 slices

pineapple salad

1 pineapple
8 mint leaves, finely sliced
2 tablespoons lime juice
½ teaspoon caster (superfine) sugar
1 teaspoon orange flower water
3 tablespoons passionfruit pulp

Slice the skin off the pineapple, cutting out any brown
'eyes'. Cut the pineapple into quarters lengthways
and remove the woody core. Finely slice the trimmed
quarters into bite-sized pieces and put them in a bowl
with the mint.

In a small bowl, mix together the lime juice, sugar,
orange flower water and passionfruit pulp. Pour
the mixture over the pineapple and lightly toss to
combine. Serves 4

banana bread with the crunch of pecans and the zing of lemon

Opposite: nutty banana bread
Over: pineapple salad

black sticky rice with fresh papaya

200 g (7 oz/1 cup) black rice
4 tablespoons grated palm sugar or soft
    brown sugar
1 teaspoon natural vanilla extract
125 ml (4 fl oz/1/2 cup) coconut milk
fresh papaya or banana slices, to serve
coconut milk, extra, for drizzling

Soak the rice in plenty of cold water for 1 hour. Drain, rinse, then drain again. Put the rice in a saucepan with 500 ml (17 fl oz/2 cups) of water. Bring to the boil, stirring occasionally, then reduce the heat to low. Cover and simmer for 35 minutes.

Stir through the sugar, vanilla extract, coconut milk and a pinch of salt. Simmer over low heat, uncovered, for a further 10 minutes, then take the rice off the heat and allow to cool. Serve with slices of fresh papaya or banana and a drizzle of coconut milk. Serves 4

tropical fruit with rosewater syrup

3 tablespoons sugar
2 tablespoons lime juice
1/4 teaspoon rosewater
1 large mango, peeled, seeded and diced
1 large red papaya, peeled, seeded and diced
12 fresh lychees, peeled, or 400 g (14 oz) tinned
    lychees, drained
shaved coconut (Basics), to serve

To make the rosewater syrup, put the sugar in a small saucepan with 125 ml (4 fl oz/1/2 cup) of water and bring to the boil. Reduce the heat and simmer for 5 minutes, stirring occasionally to ensure that the sugar melts completely. Take the pan off the heat and allow to cool completely. Stir in the lime juice and rosewater, then pour the syrup into a small glass bowl and chill in the refrigerator until ready to use.

Divide all the fruit among four bowls, scatter with slivers of shaved coconut and drizzle with some of the syrup. Serves 4

fresh berries with honey-lime yoghurt

2 tablespoons honey
juice of 1 lime
generous pinch of ground cardamom
250 g (9 oz/12/3 cups) strawberries
310 g (11 oz/2 cups) blueberries
300 g (101/2 oz/11/4 scant cups) plain or
    Greek-style yoghurt

Put the honey, lime juice and cardamom in a small saucepan and warm over low heat. Stir until the lime and honey are well combined, then remove from the heat and allow to cool.

Hull the strawberries and slice them in half, or into quarters if large. Divide the strawberries and blueberries among four bowls. Top with a large dollop of yoghurt and drizzle the honey mixture over the yoghurt. Serves 4

start the day with a bowl of exotic rice and juicy sweet papaya

black sticky rice with fresh papaya

tropical fruit with rosewater syrup

22

fresh berries with honey-lime yoghurt

23

summer nectarine 'jam'

4 large nectarines (about 600 g/1 lb 5 oz in total)
4 tablespoons sugar
1/2 vanilla bean, split
1/2 teaspoon orange flower water
8 slices nutty banana bread (page 17) or walnut
    bread (Basics), toasted and buttered

Remove the stones from the nectarines, then thickly slice the flesh and put the slices in a saucepan. Add the sugar, vanilla bean and 4 tablespoons of water. Simmer over low heat for 18–20 minutes, or until the nectarines are just beginning to break up.

Remove the vanilla bean and add the orange flower water. Serve spooned over slices of toasted and buttered banana or walnut bread. Serves 4–6

coconut muesli

400 g (14 oz/4 cups) rolled (porridge) oats
125 g (4 1/2 oz/1 cup) unsalted sunflower seeds
2 tablespoons sesame seeds
125 g (4 1/2 oz/1 cup) slivered almonds
120 g (4 1/4 oz/2 cups) shredded coconut
250 ml (9 fl oz oz/3/4 cup) maple syrup
4 tablespoons vegetable oil
40 g (1 1/2 oz/1/4 cup) finely sliced dried peaches
35 g (1 1/4 oz/1/4 cup) finely sliced dried mango

Preheat the oven to 150°C (300°F/Gas 2). Put the oats in a large bowl with the sunflower seeds, sesame seeds, almonds and coconut and mix well.

Heat the maple syrup and oil in a small saucepan over low heat. Pour the warm mixture over the muesli and stir so that all the grains and seeds are well covered.

Spread the mixture over two baking trays and bake for 30 minutes, stirring occasionally, and swapping the trays around in the oven halfway through baking. Remove from the oven and allow to cool.

Transfer to a large bowl, add the peach and mango and toss well. The muesli can be stored in an airtight container for up to 1 month. Makes about 1.2 kg (2 lb 10 oz), enough for 12 serves

jammy nectarines, buttered toast and early morning sunshine

Opposite: summer nectarine 'jam'
Over: coconut muesli

spinach and coconut soup

2 bunches English spinach (about 1 kg/
    2 lb 4 oz in total)
4 tablespoons olive oil
2 onions, finely sliced
2 garlic cloves, finely chopped
1/2 teaspoon ground cumin
500 ml (17 fl oz/2 cups) vegetable stock
400 ml (14 fl oz) tin coconut milk

Rinse the spinach under cold running water, then drain and roughly chop. Heat the olive oil in a large saucepan over medium heat. Add the onion, garlic and cumin and sauté for 5 minutes, or until the onion is soft and translucent.

Add the spinach, cover and cook for 2–3 minutes, then toss the spinach about a little so that it cooks evenly. When all the spinach has sweated down to a dark green colour, take the pan off the heat.

Put the spinach in a blender with half the stock. Blend until smooth, then return to the saucepan. Stir in the coconut milk and remaining stock and warm the soup over medium heat. Season to taste with sea salt and ground white pepper. Serves 6

green papaya and chicken salad

1 lemon grass stem, trimmed
juice of 1 lemon
1 tablespoon sea salt
2 boneless, skinless chicken breasts
2 tablespoons tamarind purée
1 teaspoon soy sauce
2 teaspoons finely grated fresh ginger
1 tablespoon grated palm sugar or soft brown sugar
1/2 teaspoon ground cumin
1 large red chilli, seeded and finely sliced
3 spring onions (scallions), finely sliced
1 large green papaya (about 650 g/1 lb 7 oz),
    peeled and seeded, flesh shredded
1 handful mint
1 handful coriander (cilantro) leaves

Put a large pot of water over high heat and bring to the boil. Cut the lemon grass stem into several pieces and add them to the pot along with the lemon juice and salt. When the water has begun to boil, add the chicken breasts, then cover the pot and take it off the heat for 40 minutes — during this time the residual heat will gently poach the chicken. Lift the chicken out of the liquid and allow to cool before shredding the meat.

Put the tamarind purée in a large non-metallic bowl and add 125 ml (4 fl oz/1/2 cup) of water. Stir to combine, then add the soy sauce, ginger, sugar, cumin and chilli. Stir until the sugar has dissolved.

Add the shredded chicken, spring onion, papaya, mint and coriander and toss to combine. Serves 4

a sprinkle of cumin and a splash of coconut milk

Opposite: spinach and coconut soup
Over: green papaya and chicken salad

chilled tomato soup

2 teaspoons sea salt
1 teaspoon ground cumin
1/2 teaspoon ground white pepper
1 tablespoon finely grated fresh ginger
2 tablespoons olive oil
10 large vine-ripened tomatoes
10 mint leaves
125 ml (4 fl oz/1/2 cup) dry sherry
small mint leaves, extra, to serve

Preheat the oven to 180°C (350°F/Gas 4). In a small bowl, combine the sea salt, cumin, white pepper, ginger and olive oil.

Using a small, sharp-pointed knife, remove the stem of one tomato with a circular action to make a crater in the top. Repeat with the other tomatoes and sit them on a baking tray. Fill the top of each tomato with the salt mixture, then bake for 30 minutes, or until they are soft and starting to split. Remove from the oven and allow to cool.

Roughly chop the tomatoes, then put them in a blender or food processor along with the mint. Blend to a purée, strain into a large bowl, then stir in the sherry. Cover with plastic wrap and chill until ready to serve. Spoon into four bowls and add a scattering of small mint leaves. Serves 4

prosciutto and mango salad

11/2 tablespoons olive oil
2 teaspoons red wine vinegar
6 kalamata olives, pitted and roughly chopped
1 teaspoon thyme leaves
100 g (31/2 oz/23/4 cups) mizuna or baby salad leaves
2 mangoes, peeled, seeded and diced
4 slices prosciutto
40 g (11/2 oz/1/3 cup) slivered almonds, toasted

Put the olive oil, vinegar, olives and thyme in a small bowl and lightly season with sea salt and freshly ground black pepper. Mix together to make a dressing and set aside.

Put the salad leaves on a serving platter, then arrange the mango over the top. Roughly tear the prosciutto into bite-sized pieces and scatter over the salad. Stir the dressing again, then drizzle it over the salad before scattering with the almonds. Serves 4

green mango salad

6 mint leaves
11/2 tablespoons lime juice
11/2 tablespoons fish sauce
1 tablespoon caster (superfine) sugar
1 small red chilli, seeded and finely chopped
3 green mangoes
2 tablespoons finely chopped roasted peanuts
1 handful coriander (cilantro) leaves
small cos (romaine) lettuce leaves or betel leaves, to serve (optional)

Finely chop the mint leaves and put them in a large non-metallic bowl with the lime juice, fish sauce, sugar and chilli. Stir until the sugar has dissolved, then set the dressing aside.

Peel the mangoes and cut the flesh away from the seed. Finely julienne or grate the flesh and add it to the dressing, along with the peanuts, coriander leaves and remaining mint. Toss to combine and serve the salad as a side dish, or on small cos lettuce or betel leaves as a refreshing starter. Serves 4 as a side dish

Opposite: chilled tomato soup
Over: prosciutto and mango salad; green mango salad

roast pork with a pineapple glaze

500 ml (17 fl oz/2 cups) pineapple juice
3 tablespoons maple syrup
2 garlic cloves, finely chopped
4 star anise
2 cinnamon sticks
3 large red chillies, seeded and cut into large pieces
1 kg (2 lb 4 oz) pork loin, skin cut off and reserved
2 tablespoons balsamic vinegar
12 thin pineapple slices, skin and core removed
green salad, to serve

Make a marinade by mixing the pineapple juice and maple syrup together in a large bowl with the garlic, star anise, cinnamon sticks and chilli. Using a sharp knife, cut 5 mm (1/4 inch) deep slashes, 4–5 cm (1 1/2–2 inches) apart, into the pork. Sit the pork in the marinade, roll it around until well coated, then cover and marinate in the refrigerator overnight.

Heat the oven to 200°C (400°F/Gas 6). Lift the pork into a roasting tin, pour the marinade all over and around the pork, then cover with foil and roast for 40 minutes.

Meanwhile, make the crackling. Score the pork skin lightly with a very sharp knife, then cut it into several strips. Put the strips in a roasting tin, brush them with water, sprinkle with salt and roast for 20 minutes, or until golden brown and crackly. Drain off any fat.

Take the foil off the pork and baste the meat with the pan juices. Roast, uncovered, for a further 30–35 minutes, or until the juices run clear when a skewer is inserted into the thickest part of the meat. Loosely cover the pork with foil and allow to rest for 10 minutes. Meanwhile, stir the vinegar into the pan juices.

Carve the pork and serve on the pineapple slices with a spoonful of pan juices, a green salad and some bits of crackling. Serves 6

duck curry with lychees

1 whole duck, rinsed and dried
1 onion, finely diced
2 garlic cloves, crushed
1 tablespoon finely grated fresh ginger
1 teaspoon chilli powder
2 tablespoons finely chopped lemon grass, white part only
1/2 teaspoon ground turmeric
2 tablespoons tamarind purée
400 ml (14 fl oz) tin coconut milk
4 makrut (kaffir lime) leaves
12 fresh lychees, peeled, or 400 g (14 oz) tinned lychees, drained
steamed white rice (Basics), to serve

Using a cleaver or heavy, sharp knife, cut the duck into 8–10 pieces, through the joints and across the breast (you could ask your butcher to do this, if you prefer). Put a wok or large saucepan over high heat and sear the duck pieces in two batches for 2–3 minutes each time, or until the skin is crispy and golden. Remove to a plate.

Reduce the heat to low and add the onion, garlic, ginger, chilli powder, lemon grass and turmeric to the wok or pan. Fry for 2 minutes, or until the onion is soft, then add the tamarind purée, coconut milk, lime leaves and 250 ml (9 fl oz/1 cup) of water. Simmer for 5 minutes.

Add the duck and simmer for 40 minutes, then add the lychees and cook for a further 5 minutes to heat through. Serve with steamed white rice. Serves 4

a tangy twist on roast pork with the bite of fresh pineapple

Opposite: roast pork with a pineapple glaze

duck curry with lychees

chicken and peppered peach salad

In a large bowl, combine 1 1/2 tablespoons white wine vinegar, 125 ml (4 fl oz/1/2 cup) olive oil and 1 1/2 teaspoons freshly ground black pepper. Slice 4 ripe peaches into the pepper dressing and lightly toss to coat. Arrange 100 g (3 1/2 oz/2 1/4 cups) baby English spinach leaves on a serving platter or in a bowl. Add the dressed peaches and 200 g (7 oz/2 cups) shredded roast chicken meat and season with a little sea salt. Serves 4

watermelon and feta salad

Take a 750 g (1 lb 10 oz) portion of seedless watermelon, cut away the rind, then cut the flesh into bite-sized chunks. Cut 200 g (7 oz) Bulgarian feta cheese into 2 cm (3/4 inch) cubes. Roughly pile the feta and watermelon onto a serving platter, then scatter 20 pitted and sliced kalamata olives, 12 finely sliced mint leaves and 2 finely diced celery stalks over the top. Mix together 1 tablespoon red wine vinegar and 2 tablespoons olive oil and pour over the salad. Season with freshly ground black pepper. Serves 4

chicken with coconut sambal

To make the coconut sambal, heat 2 teaspoons vegetable oil in a frying pan over medium heat. Add 1 tablespoon finely chopped lemon grass (white part only), 1 seeded and finely chopped large red chilli and 1/2 finely diced onion. Cook, stirring, for 5 minutes. Reduce the heat to low and stir in 3 tablespoons desiccated coconut, 1 teaspoon dark brown sugar and 1/2 teaspoon sea salt. Cook, stirring, for 5 minutes, or until golden and crisp. Take off the heat and allow to cool. Shred 2 poached boneless, skinless chicken breasts, put them in a bowl and mix through 3 tablespoons olive oil and 1 tablespoon lime juice. Pile 100 g (3 1/2 oz/2 1/4 cups) baby English spinach leaves on a serving platter. Arrange 1 sliced large red papaya over the top, add the chicken and sprinkle with the coconut sambal. Serves 4

orange and watercress salad

Very finely slice 1/2 red onion, put it in a sieve over a bowl and sprinkle with 1 teaspoon sea salt. Using a sharp knife, cut the top and bottom off 4 oranges. Stand the oranges on a chopping board and slice away the skin and pith. Working over a large bowl to catch the juices, remove the segments by running a knife between each membrane. Put the segments in the bowl with the captured orange juice, 2 handfuls of picked watercress sprigs and 20 niçoise olives. Mix well. Rinse the onion slices, then press between paper towels to squeeze out any excess liquid. Put them in a small bowl and pour over 1 tablespoon red wine vinegar. Arrange the orange salad on a serving platter, then scatter over the vinegary onion and drizzle with 2 tablespoons extra virgin olive oil. Serves 4

41

roast pork with mango chutney

1 tablespoon olive oil
1 red onion, finely diced
1 tablespoon finely grated fresh ginger
2 tablespoons finely chopped lemon grass,
    white part only
2 tablespoons tamarind purée
125 ml (4 fl oz/1/2 cup) white wine vinegar
115 g (4 oz/1/2 cup) dark brown sugar
1 large red chilli, seeded and finely chopped
2 just-ripe mangoes, peeled, seeded and diced
1.5 kg (3 lb 5 oz) pork shoulder, skin scored
    (ask your butcher to do this)
green salad, to serve

To make the mango chutney, heat the olive oil in a saucepan over medium heat and add the onion, ginger and lemon grass. Cook, stirring, for 10–12 minutes, or until the onion is slightly caramelized. Stir in the tamarind purée, vinegar, sugar, chilli and mango. Bring to the boil, then reduce the heat and simmer for 20 minutes. Set aside.

Meanwhile, preheat the oven to 220°C (425°F/Gas 7). Pat the pork dry with paper towels and rub the scored skin well with salt. Season with freshly ground black pepper. Sit the pork in a roasting tin, skin side up, and roast for 25 minutes, then turn the oven temperature down to 180°C (350°F/Gas 4) and cook for a further 1 hour. To test if the meat is done, insert a sharp knife or skewer into the centre — the juices should run clear.

Transfer the pork to a warm serving platter, cover with foil and leave to rest for 15 minutes. If the skin isn't quite crunchy and needs further cooking, slice it off using a sharp knife, put it back in the roasting tin and roast on the top shelf of the oven for a few minutes. Carve the pork and serve with the mango chutney and a green salad. Serves 6

chicken salad with fresh coconut

2 tablespoons finely chopped lemon grass,
    white part only
1 teaspoon grated palm sugar or soft brown sugar
200 ml (7 fl oz) coconut milk
3 tablespoons lime juice
1 teaspoon sesame oil
2 boneless, skinless chicken breasts
1 handful mint
1/4 fresh coconut, flesh shaved (Basics)
100 g (31/2 oz) snow pea (mangetout) shoots
2 Lebanese (short) cucumbers, finely sliced
2 tablespoons sesame seeds, toasted
lime wedges, to serve

Preheat the oven to 180°C (350°F/Gas 4). Make a dressing by putting the lemon grass, sugar, coconut milk and 2 tablespoons of the lime juice in a saucepan over low heat. Simmer for 5 minutes, stirring occasionally to ensure the sugar dissolves, then take the pan off the heat and allow the dressing to cool.

Put the sesame oil and remaining lime juice in a small baking dish. Add the chicken breasts and toss well to coat, then cover with foil and bake for 30 minutes. Remove the chicken from the oven and let it cool completely, keeping the baking dish covered.

Roughly shred the chicken and stir it through the dressing. Add the mint, coconut, snow pea shoots, cucumber and sesame seeds and toss together well. Serve with lime wedges. Serves 4

sweet pork, golden crackling, lemon grass and mango

Opposite: roast pork with mango chutney

chicken salad with fresh coconut

roasted duck breast salad

2 tablespoons dark brown sugar
$^1/_4$ teaspoon Chinese five-spice
1 teaspoon sea salt
4 boneless duck breasts, skin on
$^1/_2$ teaspoon sichuan peppercorns
100 g ($3^1/_2$ oz/$2^3/_4$ cups) mizuna, mesclun
    or baby salad leaves
2 mangoes, peeled, seeded and sliced
2 spring onions (scallions), finely sliced
    on the diagonal
2 tablespoons Chinese black vinegar

Preheat the oven to 180°C (350°F/Gas 4). In a small
bowl, combine the sugar, five-spice and sea salt.
Using a sharp knife, lightly score the skin of the duck
breasts in a crisscross pattern, then rub the sugar
mixture into the duck skin.

Heat a non-stick frying pan over high heat and sear
the duck breasts, skin side down, for a few minutes,
or until crisp — the skin will go quite dark as the sugar
caramelizes. Put the duck breasts, skin side up, on a
rack set over a baking tray and roast for 15 minutes.
Remove the tray from the oven, cover with foil and
allow the duck to rest for a few minutes.

Roughly grind the peppercorns using a mortar and
pestle. Arrange the salad leaves, mango and spring
onion on four serving plates. Finely slice the duck
breasts diagonally across the grain and arrange over
the salad. Drizzle the duck with the Chinese black
vinegar and sprinkle with the ground peppercorns.
Serves 4

roasted duck breast salad

macerated plums with coconut sorbet

macerated plums with coconut sorbet

145 g (5 oz/^{2}/$_3$ cup) caster (superfine) sugar
1 vanilla bean
250 ml (9 fl oz/1 cup) milk
400 ml (14 fl oz) tin coconut milk
1 tablespoon golden rum
10 blood plums (about 800 g/1 lb 12 oz in total)
2 tablespoons dark brown sugar
juice of 1 orange

Put the caster sugar, vanilla bean and 150 ml (5 fl oz) of water in a saucepan over medium heat. Stir well to dissolve the sugar. When the syrup comes to the boil, let it bubble for 10 minutes. Discard the vanilla bean and pour the syrup into a bowl.

To make the coconut sorbet, pour the milk and coconut milk into the saucepan and let it warm through. Take the pan off the heat, stir in the vanilla syrup and rum, then allow to cool. Churn the mixture in an ice cream machine, or pour it into a shallow container, place it in the freezer, then stir every hour until the sorbet freezes.

Cut the plums into thick slices, removing the stones as you go. Put the plums in a bowl, add the dark brown sugar and orange juice and toss until well coated. Cover and refrigerate for 1 hour. Divide the chilled plums among six bowls and serve with the coconut sorbet. Serves 6

very vanilla peach meringues

4 egg whites
230 g (8 oz/1 cup) caster (superfine) sugar
2 vanilla beans
^{1}/$_2$ teaspoon natural vanilla extract
6 peaches, stones removed, cut in half
250 ml (9 fl oz/1 cup) dessert wine
3 tablespoons raw caster (superfine) sugar
300 ml (10^1/$_2$ fl oz) crème fraîche or thick
    (double/heavy) cream

Preheat the oven to 110°C (225°F/Gas ^{1}/$_2$). Line two large baking trays with baking paper.

Whisk the egg whites until stiff but not dry. Gradually whisk in half the caster sugar, whisking until very shiny, then add the remaining caster sugar and lightly whisk until incorporated. Split a vanilla bean along its length, scrape out the seeds with the tip of a knife and stir them into the egg whites, along with the vanilla extract.

Spoon the mixture onto the baking trays to form six 10–12 cm (4–4^1/$_2$ inch) rounds. Bake for 1^1/$_2$ hours, or until crisp and golden. Turn the oven off, open the door slightly and leave the meringues to cool. When cool enough to handle, peel the meringues off the baking paper and put them on a rack to cool.

Turn the oven temperature up to 210°C (415°F/Gas 6–7). Put the peaches, cut side up, in a single layer in a baking dish. Pour the wine over the top and sprinkle with the raw sugar. Split the remaining vanilla bean in half, cut it into thirds and add to the baking dish. Bake for 15 minutes, or until the peaches are soft and slightly caramelized on top. Remove from the oven and allow to cool.

Divide the meringues among six serving plates and top with a dollop of crème fraîche or cream. Add two peach halves to each plate and drizzle with the syrup from the baking dish. Garnish with the vanilla bean pieces. Serves 6

dip your spoon in sweetly seductive coconut ice

very vanilla peach meringues

honey-spiced parfait with fresh berries

5 egg yolks
100 g (3¹/2 oz) caster (superfine) sugar
2 tablespoons honey
¹/4 teaspoon ground cardamom
500 ml (17 fl oz/2 cups) crème fraîche or sour cream
fresh berries, such as raspberries, blackberries
    or strawberries, to serve

Using a whisk or electric beaters, whisk the egg yolks, sugar and honey in a large bowl until thick and pale.

Gently fold the cardamom and crème fraîche through, then spoon into an 8 x 22 cm (3¹/4 x 8¹/2 inch) loaf (bar) tin lined with baking paper. Freeze overnight, or until firm.

Cut the parfait into six thick slices and serve with fresh berries. Serves 6

passionfruit jelly with fresh mango

8–10 passionfruit
300 ml (10¹/2 fl oz) pineapple juice
140 g (5 oz/²/3 cup) sugar
2 tablespoons lime juice
6 gelatine leaves
2 ripe mangoes
cream (whipping), to serve

Cut each passionfruit in half. Using a spoon, scoop the pulp into a sieve over a bowl. Using the same spoon, work the seeds into the sieve to extract as much juice as possible — you will need 60 ml (2 fl oz/¹/4 cup) of passionfruit juice for the jelly.

Put the pineapple juice and sugar in a saucepan with 200 ml (7 fl oz) of water and stir over medium heat until the sugar has dissolved. Take the pan off the heat and stir in the passionfruit juice and lime juice. Pour 600 ml (21 fl oz) of the liquid into a large measuring cup.

Fill a large bowl with cold water and soak the gelatine leaves for a few minutes, or until they have dissolved to a jellied consistency. Squeeze the excess water from the gelatine leaves and add them to the warm fruit juice mixture. Stir to ensure that the gelatine is completely dissolved, then pour into a bowl. Cover with plastic wrap and refrigerate for several hours until firm, or overnight.

Remove the skin and stones from the mangoes and roughly chop the flesh into bite-sized pieces. Layer spoonfuls of the jelly and mango in six chilled serving glasses and serve with cream. Serves 6

a sumptuous mouthful of summer berries and velvety cream

Opposite: honey-spiced parfait with fresh berries
Over: passionfruit jelly with fresh mango

rosy plum crumbles

rosy plum crumbles

10 blood plums (about 800 g/1 lb 12 oz in total)
80 g (2³/4 oz/¹/3 cup) caster (superfine) sugar
1 teaspoon rosewater
115 g (4 oz/¹/2 cup) dark brown sugar
60 g (2¹/4 oz/¹/2 cup) plain (all-purpose) flour
45 g (1¹/2 oz/¹/2 cup) desiccated coconut
75 g (2¹/2 oz) unsalted butter
whipped cream or thick (double/heavy) cream,
    to serve

Preheat the oven to 180°C (350°F/Gas 4). Slice the plums, removing the stones, and put them in a bowl. Add the caster sugar and rosewater and toss until the plums are well coated in sugar. Set aside for 10 minutes.

Toss the brown sugar, flour and coconut together in a bowl. Rub the butter in with your fingertips until the mixture resembles breadcrumbs. Set aside.

Stir the plums again to ensure they are well coated, then divide among six 150 ml (5 fl oz) ovenproof bowls, piling the plums above the top of the bowls as they will cook down quite a bit.

Top the plums with the coconut mixture, then sit the bowls on a baking tray and bake for 30 minutes, or until the crumbles are golden and the juices are bubbling over the sides of the bowls. Serve warm with cream. Serves 6

peachy fruit salad

Cut 4 peaches in half and remove the stones and skins. Slice the peaches into a bowl. Add 2 sliced bananas and the pulp of 4 passionfruit. Cover with the juice of 2 oranges and sprinkle with 1 tablespoon caster (superfine) sugar. Lightly stir to just coat the fruit in the sweet juice. Serve with ice cream, sorbet or creamy yoghurt. Serves 4

rum and pineapple ice

Put 55 g (2 oz/1/4 cup) caster (superfine) sugar and 500 ml (17 fl oz/2 cups) pineapple juice in a saucepan over medium heat. Stir until the sugar has dissolved, then remove from the heat and stir in 1 teaspoon natural vanilla extract and 100 ml (3 1/2 fl oz) golden rum. Pour the liquid into a wide shallow container and freeze for 4–5 hours, or until frozen. Remove from the freezer and allow to soften, then break the mixture up using a fork until it looks like crushed ice. Return to the freezer until ready to serve. Spoon into four chilled parfait glasses and drizzle each with 2 tablespoons coconut milk. Serves 4

warm peaches with cinnamon cream

To make the cinnamon cream, put 3 tablespoons plain yoghurt in a bowl with 1/4 teaspoon ground cinnamon, 1/2 teaspoon natural vanilla extract and 1 teaspoon caster (superfine) sugar. Stir until the sugar has dissolved. Fold through 150 ml (5 fl oz) whipped cream, then cover with plastic wrap and chill until ready to serve. Cut 4 ripe peaches in half and remove the stones. Sit the peaches on a tray, cut side up, and sprinkle with 4 tablespoons raw caster (superfine) sugar or light brown sugar. Cook under a hot grill (broiler) for 10 minutes, or until the sugar is beginning to darken. Serve with the cinnamon cream and some pistachio biscotti (Basics), cardamom almond bread (Basics) or sweet wafers. Serves 4

lemon grass granita

Cut 2 trimmed lemon grass stems into thirds and bruise them with the handle of a heavy knife. Put them in a saucepan with 145 g (5 1/4 oz/2/3 cup) caster (superfine) sugar and 500 ml (17 fl oz/2 cups) water. Bring to the boil, reduce the heat and simmer for 5 minutes. Take off the heat and allow to cool. Stir in 250 ml (9 fl oz/1 cup) pineapple juice, the juice of 2 limes and 100 ml (3 1/2 fl oz) vodka. Strain into a wide, shallow container and freeze for 1 hour. Using a fork, scrape the ice from the edges back into the liquid. Return to the freezer and repeat another three times, until the granita looks like crushed ice. Slice the flesh of 1/2 small, ripe pineapple into thin wedges and divide among serving plates. Serve the granita on the side, in chilled glasses. Serves 4–6

leaf

leafy greens   bowls of goodness

herbs and citrus   flavour and crunch

There's something about a big bowl of leafy greens that makes me feel instantly healthy. I just know I'm doing myself a favour by eating them and nowadays, with supermarket aisles brimming with hand-picked baby leaves, bundles of herbs and so many different varieties of lettuce, there is no excuse not to enjoy a lavish bowl of salad. Add a few wonderful flavours and a good splash of dressing and you really do have food of the gods. This chapter follows the no longer humble salad as it heads off on an adventure, having close encounters with delectable duck, chicken and golden roast vegetables.

prosciutto with papaya and basil

juice of 1 orange
1 teaspoon red wine vinegar
3 tablespoons olive oil
2 small red papayas
6 slices prosciutto
15 small basil leaves

Put the orange juice, vinegar and olive oil in a small bowl and mix together to make a dressing.

Cut each papaya into quarters and remove the seeds and skin. Cut the flesh into bite-sized pieces and arrange them on a serving platter. Tear the prosciutto into bite-sized bits and scatter them over the papaya. Scatter the basil leaves over the top.

Stir the dressing again, drizzle over the salad and sprinkle with freshly ground black pepper. Serves 4

bocconcini salad

1 tablespoon white wine vinegar
4 tablespoons extra virgin olive oil
20 mint leaves, roughly chopped
1 handful flat-leaf (Italian) parsley, roughly chopped
350 g (12 oz/2 bunches) thin asparagus spears, trimmed
200 g (7 oz) bocconcini (fresh baby mozzarella cheese), cut in half
2 avocados

Put the vinegar, olive oil, mint and parsley in a large bowl.

Bring a saucepan of water to the boil. Add the asparagus spears and blanch for 1 minute, or until they begin to turn emerald green. Rinse the spears under cold running water, then cut them into 4 cm (1 1/2 inch) lengths. Add them to the mint and parsley, along with the bocconcini.

Slice the avocados in half and remove the stones. Cut the flesh into bite-sized chunks or wedges and add them to the salad. Season with sea salt and freshly ground black pepper, then gently toss before serving. Serves 4

a fresh, lively salad for hot days and balmy nights

Opposite: prosciutto with papaya and basil

bocconcini salad

smoked salmon with vegetable salad

1 fennel bulb
2 zucchini (courgettes)
2 Lebanese (short) cucumbers
1 teaspoon finely chopped mint
1 teaspoon finely chopped dill
1 tablespoon olive oil
2 tablespoons lemon juice
1 teaspoon caster (superfine) sugar
1/2 teaspoon sea salt
16 slices smoked salmon

Trim the base of the fennel, slice the bulb as finely as possible and put it in a bowl. Slice the zucchini and cucumbers as finely as possible, cutting them on the diagonal, and add them to the fennel. Add the mint, dill, olive oil, lemon juice, sugar and sea salt. Toss to combine, then set aside for 10 minutes.

Divide the smoked salmon slices among four plates. Toss the salad one more time before piling it on top of the salmon. Serves 4

chilled cucumber soup

4 Lebanese (short) cucumbers
    (about 600 g/1 lb 5 oz in total)
250 g (9 oz/1 cup) plain yoghurt
250 ml (9 fl oz/1 cup) chicken stock
3 tablespoons fine semolina
1 tablespoon lemon juice
1 tablespoon finely chopped dill
4 dill sprigs, extra, to serve

Peel three of the cucumbers, and, if you like, slice the fourth into very thin rounds to garnish the soup.

Roughly chop the peeled cucumbers and put them in a food processor with the yoghurt, stock and semolina. Blend to a smooth soup. Pour into a large pitcher, stir in the lemon juice and chopped dill and season to taste. Cover with plastic wrap and refrigerate for several hours, or until well chilled. If you like, serve garnished with the cucumber rounds and extra dill sprigs.
Serves 4

spinach and chickpea salad

2 bunches English spinach (about 1 kg/
    2 lb 4 oz in total)
2 tablespoons olive oil
1 garlic clove, crushed
400 g (14 oz) tin chickpeas, rinsed and drained
2 tablespoons sumac
1 tablespoon red wine vinegar
4 tablespoons extra virgin olive oil
45 g (1 1/2 oz/1/2 cup) desiccated coconut, toasted

Trim the spinach and rinse the leaves well under running water. Drain well. Put a heavy-based saucepan over medium heat and add the olive oil and garlic. Finely chop the spinach, add it to the saucepan and cook for a few minutes, just until all the leaves turn a dark emerald green and are softly wilted.

Drain the spinach in a colander to remove any excess liquid, then put it in a large bowl with the chickpeas, sumac, vinegar and olive oil. Toss well to coat the spinach and chickpeas, then add the coconut. Season to taste with sea salt and freshly ground black pepper. Toss again before serving. Serves 4–6

velvety salmon, crisp fennel and bitey herbs

Opposite: smoked salmon with vegetable salad
Over: chilled cucumber soup; spinach and chickpea salad

labneh salad

600 g (1 lb 5 oz) plain yoghurt
1 teaspoon salt
2 garlic cloves, crushed
8 lemon thyme sprigs
extra virgin olive oil, for drizzling
50 g (1³/₄ oz/¹/₄ cup) burghul (bulgur)
2 tablespoons finely chopped preserved lemon rind
1 handful flat-leaf (Italian) parsley, roughly chopped
100 g (3¹/₂ oz/1 heaped cup) flaked almonds, toasted
50 g (1³/₄ oz/1¹/₂ cups) wild rocket (arugula) leaves
toasted pide (Turkish/flat bread), to serve

You can buy labneh in some speciality stores but if you have the time there is something quite satisfying about making your own.

Start by mixing the yoghurt with the salt. Line a sieve with two layers of muslin (cheesecloth) and put it over a bowl. Pour the yoghurt into the sieve, then cover and allow to drain for 2 days in the refrigerator — it should now be very thick and creamy.

Roll the mixture into eight plum-sized balls and sit them in a wide container along with the garlic. Scatter with the thyme sprigs and drizzle with olive oil. Cover and leave to marinate in the refrigerator for 1 more day.

Just before serving time, put the burghul in a bowl and cover with 4 tablespoons of boiling water. Allow to sit for 5 minutes, or until all the water is absorbed. Add the preserved lemon, parsley, almonds and rocket, toss well, then divide among four plates. Top each with two labneh and drizzle with a little more olive oil. Season with sea salt and freshly ground black pepper and serve with toasted pide. Serves 4

roast duck and sweet potato salad

700 g (1 lb 9 oz) orange sweet potatoes
2 tablespoons light olive oil
1 whole Chinese roasted duck
2 tablespoons tamarind purée
1 tablespoon finely grated fresh ginger
2 tablespoons grated palm sugar or soft brown sugar
2 tablespoons lime juice
4 tablespoons olive oil
50 g (1³/₄ oz/1¹/₂ cups) wild rocket (arugula) leaves
50 g (1³/₄ oz/1¹/₂ cups) small tatsoi leaves
3 large red chillies, seeded and finely sliced

Preheat the oven to 180°C (350°F/Gas 4). Peel the sweet potatoes and cut them into bite-sized chunks. Put them on a baking tray and rub with the light olive oil. Season with sea salt and freshly ground black pepper and roast for 30 minutes, or until tender.

Remove the skin from the duck and, using a pair of kitchen scissors, cut it into thin strips. Put the strips on a baking tray and into the hot oven for 10 minutes, or until the skin begins to crisp. Remove and drain on paper towels.

Put the tamarind purée in a large bowl and add 4 tablespoons of water. Add the ginger, sugar, lime juice and olive oil and stir well to make a dressing.

Pull the flesh from the duck and roughly shred it. Add it to the tamarind dressing along with the crispy duck skin and baked sweet potato. Lightly toss, then add the rocket and tatsoi leaves. Pile the salad into six bowls, or arrange over a serving platter, and scatter with the chilli slices. Serves 6

a lunch with a leafy punch and a middle-eastern twist

Opposite: labneh salad
Over: roast duck and sweet potato salad

seared lamb with almond salad

50 g (1³/₄ oz/heaped ¹/₂ cup) flaked almonds,
    toasted and finely chopped
1 garlic clove, crushed
1 handful flat-leaf (Italian) parsley, roughly chopped
10 basil leaves, roughly chopped
3 ripe roma (plum) tomatoes, finely chopped
¹/₄ red onion, finely diced
3 tablespoons extra virgin olive oil
2 x 300 g (10¹/₂ oz) lamb backstraps or loin fillets,
    trimmed
1 tablespoon olive oil

To make the almond salad, put the almonds, garlic,
parsley, basil, tomato, onion and extra virgin olive oil
in a bowl and season liberally with sea salt and freshly
ground black pepper. Toss to combine and set aside.

Put the lamb fillets in a bowl with the olive oil and
toss a few times to thoroughly coat the lamb. Heat a
non-stick frying pan over high heat and cook the lamb
fillets for 3 minutes on each side. Transfer to a plate,
season with sea salt, cover loosely with foil and allow
to rest for a few minutes.

Spoon the almond salad into the centre of four plates.
Slice the lamb fillets on the diagonal, arrange the
slices over the salad and pour any meat juices from
the resting over the top. Serves 4

aromatic roast chicken breasts

1 vanilla bean
2 tablespoons soy sauce
2 tablespoons grated palm sugar or soft brown sugar
2 tablespoons grated lemon zest
4 boneless chicken breasts, skin on
juice of 4 lemons
4 tablespoons olive oil
50 g (1³/₄ oz) snow pea (mangetout) shoots
herbed couscous (Basics), to serve

Preheat the oven to 200°C (400°F/Gas 6). Using a
sharp knife, slice the vanilla bean in half lengthways
and scrape the seeds into a bowl (reserve the vanilla
pod for another use). Add the soy sauce, sugar and
lemon zest and stir to combine.

Using a sharp knife, cut several long incisions into the
skin of each chicken breast, then rub the soy mixture
into the skin. Put the lemon juice and olive oil in a small
casserole dish or baking dish and add the chicken
breasts, skin side up. Roast for 15 minutes, or until
the chicken is cooked through.

Carve each chicken breast into several thick slices.
Serve with the snow pea shoots on a bed of herbed
couscous, with the baking juices spooned over the
top. Serves 4

seared lamb fillets set adrift on a sea of flavour

Opposite: seared lamb with almond salad
Over: aromatic roast chicken breasts

crab and green bean salad

50 g (1³/₄ oz/¹/₃ cup) peanuts
2 tablespoons grated palm sugar or
    soft brown sugar
2 tablespoons fish sauce
4 tablespoons lime juice
2 spring onions (scallions), thinly sliced
2 large red chillies, seeded and finely sliced
1 tablespoon finely chopped lemon grass,
    white part only
200 g (7 oz) green beans, trimmed, blanched
    and sliced on the diagonal
150 g (5¹/₂ oz/1²/₃ cups) bean sprouts
150 g (5¹/₂ oz/1¹/₂ cups) fresh crabmeat
1 handful coriander (cilantro), roughly chopped
10 mint leaves, roughly chopped

Put the peanuts in a small saucepan over medium
heat and dry-fry for 2–3 minutes, or until they turn
golden brown. Take them off the heat to cool a little,
then put them in a blender or food processor and
blend until finely chopped.

Put the sugar, fish sauce and lime juice in a large
bowl and stir until the sugar has dissolved. Add all
the remaining ingredients, including the toasted
peanuts, and toss well. Serves 4

crab and green bean salad

sesame duck salad

1 whole Chinese roasted duck
600 g (1 lb 5 oz) Chinese cabbage, finely sliced
2 handfuls parsley, roughly chopped
20 mint leaves, finely chopped
1 red capsicum (pepper), finely diced
8 spring onions (scallions), finely sliced
2 tablespoons Chinese black vinegar
2 tablespoons olive oil
1 teaspoon sesame oil
1 teaspoon soy sauce
4 tablespoons sesame seeds

Remove the skin from the duck and, using a pair of kitchen scissors, cut it into thin strips. Put the strips on a baking tray and cook under a hot grill (broiler) for 2–3 minutes, or until crisp. Remove and drain on paper towels.

Pull the flesh from the duck and finely shred it. Toss it in a large bowl with the crispy duck skin, cabbage, parsley, mint, capsicum and spring onion.

In a small bowl, mix together the vinegar, olive oil, sesame oil and soy sauce, then pour over the salad. Toss well, then pile onto a serving platter or into individual bowls.

Put the sesame seeds in a small frying pan over medium heat. As soon as they start to turn golden, take them off the heat and spoon them over the salad. Serves 4–6

fragrant lime and lemon grass chicken

zest and juice of 2 limes
16 cm (6¼ inch) piece of lemon grass, trimmed
    and roughly chopped
2 garlic cloves, peeled
1 tablespoon roughly chopped fresh ginger
2 large red chillies, seeded
1 tablespoon soy sauce
4 boneless, skinless chicken breasts
2 tablespoons olive oil
100 g (3½ oz/2¾ cups) mixed salad leaves
2 handfuls coriander (cilantro) sprigs
2 tablespoons peanuts, toasted and roughly
    chopped

Preheat the oven to 200°C (400°F/Gas 6). Using a food processor or mortar and pestle, grind the lime zest, lemon grass, garlic, ginger, chilli and soy sauce into a smooth paste.

Rub the paste all over the chicken breasts and sit them in a deep baking tray. Drizzle with the olive oil and lime juice, season with a little sea salt, then cover with foil and bake for 20 minutes. Check that the chicken is cooked through using the pointed end of a sharp knife. Bake a little longer if it is still a little pink.

Remove the chicken from the oven and leave to cool (reserve the juices in the pan). Arrange the salad leaves, coriander and peanuts on four plates. Finely slice the chicken, scatter it over the salad and drizzle with the pan juices. Serves 4

sweet, flavoursome roasted duck with fragrant herbs

Opposite: sesame duck salad
Over: fragrant lime and lemon grass chicken

lamb salad with walnut pesto

1 handful basil
1 handful flat-leaf (Italian) parsley
50 g (1¾ oz/½ cup) grated parmesan cheese
1 garlic clove
100 g (3½ oz/1 cup) walnuts
170 ml (5½ fl oz/⅔ cup) olive oil
250 g (9 oz) cherry tomatoes or truss tomatoes
2 x 300 g (10½ oz) lamb backstraps or loin
   fillets, trimmed
2 baby cos (romaine) lettuces, cut into quarters

Preheat the oven to 180°C (350°F/Gas 4). Put the basil, parsley, parmesan, garlic and walnuts in a food processor with the olive oil and blend to a chunky pesto. Transfer to a bowl and season to taste with sea salt and freshly ground black pepper.

Put the whole tomatoes on a baking tray and roast for 10 minutes, or until they start to split.

Heat a heavy-based frying pan over high heat and sear the lamb fillets for 2 minutes on each side. Put them on a baking tray and bake for 5 minutes, then transfer to a plate, season with sea salt, cover loosely with foil and leave to rest for 5 minutes.

Divide the lettuce quarters among four warmed plates. Slice the lamb on the diagonal and arrange over the lettuce, then top with the roasted tomatoes and a large spoonful of the pesto. Serve drizzled with a little of the pesto oil. Serves 4

fried tofu salad

300 g (10½ oz) firm tofu
60 g (2¼ oz/½ cup) plain (all-purpose) flour
1 teaspoon sea salt
1 tablespoon sesame seeds
125 ml (4 fl oz/½ cup) peanut oil
2 Lebanese (short) cucumbers, peeled and diced
4 spring onions (scallions), finely sliced on the
   diagonal
2 ripe roma (plum) tomatoes, diced
1 handful coriander (cilantro) leaves
20 mint leaves, finely chopped
1 tablespoon lime juice
2 tablespoons kecap manis

Sit the tofu on paper towels for 30 minutes to soak up any excess liquid.

Put the flour in a hot frying pan over high heat and toast it, stirring, for 2½ minutes, or until it turns golden brown. Tip the toasted flour into a large bowl and allow to cool, then stir in the sea salt and sesame seeds. Cut the tofu into 12 slices about 5 mm (¼ inch) thick and toss them in the toasted flour mixture.

Heat the peanut oil in a frying pan and fry the tofu over medium–high heat for 2 minutes on each side, or until golden brown — you may need to do this in two batches. Leave to drain on paper towels, then cut each tofu slice into three triangles, or leave in larger slices.

Gently toss the tofu in a bowl with the cucumber, spring onion, tomato, coriander and mint. Season to taste with sea salt.

In a small bowl, mix together the lime juice and kecap manis. Drizzle over the salad and toss once again before serving. Serves 4

juicy pink lamb, tiny roast tomatoes and a nutty crunch

Opposite: lamb salad with walnut pesto

fried tofu salad

ma hor on betel leaves

Put 2 roughly chopped garlic cloves in a blender or food processor with 1 handful coriander (cilantro) leaves, 1/2 teaspoon drained green peppercorns in brine, 1 teaspoon finely grated fresh ginger, 2 finely chopped spring onions (scallions) and 2 tablespoons peanut oil. Blend to a smooth paste. Heat a frying pan over medium heat, add the herb paste and cook for 2 minutes. Add 150 g (5 1/2 oz) minced (ground) pork and 75 g (2 1/2 oz/1 cup) prawn (shrimp) meat and cook, stirring, for 5 minutes, or until the meat has coloured. Add 2 finely sliced makrut (kaffir lime) leaves, 1 1/2 tablespoons grated palm sugar or soft brown sugar and 1 1/2 tablespoons fish sauce. Reduce the heat and cook for 2–3 minutes, or until slightly sticky. Allow to cool, then spoon onto 20 fresh betel leaves, about 1 tablespoon at a time. Makes 20

tuna salad in lettuce cups

Bring a saucepan of water to the boil and add 2 eggs at room temperature. Simmer for 5 minutes, then remove the eggs and leave to cool. In a bowl, whisk 1 teaspoon red wine vinegar with 1 teaspoon dijon mustard, then slowly whisk in 3 tablespoons olive oil. Peel and finely chop the eggs, then add them to the dressing with 3 tablespoons finely grated parmesan cheese, 100 g (3 1/2 oz) drained tinned tuna, 1 diced celery stalk, 10 roughly chopped pitted kalamata olives and 2 handfuls flat-leaf (Italian) parsley, roughly chopped. Season to taste and stir to combine. Cut 10 cherry tomatoes into quarters. Spoon a heaped teaspoon of the salad into 20 small mignonette lettuce leaves and garnish with the cherry tomato quarters. Makes 20

capsicum relish on baby cos

To make the capsicum relish, roast 3 whole red capsicums (peppers) in a hot oven or over a gas flame until the skins are charred and black. Put them in a bowl, cover with plastic wrap and leave to cool. Peel away the seeds, membranes and blackened skin, then finely dice the flesh and place in a bowl. Add 2 tablespoons finely diced red onion, 2 tablespoons currants, 15 finely sliced mint leaves, 15 finely sliced basil leaves, 2 tablespoons extra virgin olive oil and 1 teaspoon balsamic vinegar. Gently mix together and season to taste. Wash and dry 20 small cos (romaine) lettuce leaves. Spoon a heaped teaspoon of the capsicum relish into each leaf, then crumble 70 g (2½ oz) goat's cheese over the top. Makes 20

san choy bau

Remove the core and all the dark outer leaves from 2 iceberg lettuces. Carefully uncurl the inner leaves, keeping them in neat cups, then rinse in a large bowl of cold water and drain. Heat 2 tablespoons peanut oil and 2 teaspoons sesame oil in a large non-stick frying pan over medium–high heat. Add 500 g (1 lb 2 oz) minced (ground) pork and cook, stirring, for 8 minutes, or until lightly golden. Stir in 2 tablespoons grated fresh ginger, 8 finely sliced spring onions (scallions), 2 tablespoons soy sauce, 2 tablespoons hoisin sauce and 200 g (7 oz/1¼ cups) chopped water chestnuts. Cook for 2 minutes, then stir in 1 handful coriander (cilantro) leaves. Serve in a warmed bowl, with the lettuce leaf cups on a side plate. Serves 4

lamb skewers with herbed yoghurt

300 g (10½ oz/about 2¼ cups) plain yoghurt
2 spring onions (scallions), finely sliced
1 teaspoon garam masala
1 teaspoon grated fresh ginger
1 garlic clove, crushed
½ teaspoon ground turmeric
½ teaspoon chilli powder
300 g (10½ oz) diced lamb, cut into 3 cm
    (1¼ inch) cubes
15 mint leaves, finely chopped
25 g (1 oz/1 bunch) chives, finely snipped
baby leaf salad (optional), to serve

Spoon 4 tablespoons of the yoghurt into a bowl and add the spring onion, garam masala, ginger, garlic, turmeric and chilli powder. Stir to combine, then add the lamb, mixing well to ensure all the cubes are well coated. Cover and refrigerate overnight.

One hour before cooking, soak 8 wooden skewers in cold water to prevent scorching.

Mix the remaining yoghurt with the mint and chives, then spoon into four little serving dishes. Thread the lamb onto the soaked skewers and cook on a hot barbecue chargrill plate or chargrill pan for 4 minutes on each side, or until cooked to your liking. Remove from the heat and season with sea salt. Serve with little dishes of the herbed yoghurt and perhaps a baby leaf salad. Serves 4

fried shallot and cashew salad

125 ml (4 fl oz/½ cup) peanut oil
12 French or red Asian shallots, peeled and cut in half
2 large red chillies, seeded and finely chopped
2 garlic cloves
½ teaspoon sea salt
1 tablespoon grated palm sugar or soft brown sugar
2 tablespoons fish sauce
2 Lebanese (short) cucumbers, peeled and diced
250 g (9 oz) cherry tomatoes, cut into quarters
125 g (4½ oz/heaped ¾ cup) cashew nuts,
    toasted and roughly chopped
2 handfuls Thai basil
2 handfuls coriander (cilantro) leaves

Heat the peanut oil in a frying pan over high heat. When the oil begins to shimmer, add the shallots and fry, stirring, for 1½ minutes, or until golden brown. Remove and drain on paper towels.

In a mortar and pestle or small food processor, pound the chilli, garlic and sea salt into a paste. Add the sugar and work it into the paste for about 1 minute, then stir in the fish sauce to make a dressing.

Put the shallots in a large bowl with the cucumber, tomatoes, cashews, basil and coriander. Pour the dressing over and toss to combine. Serve as a side dish with grilled chicken or seared beef. Serves 4

roast pumpkin and tofu salad

700 g (1 lb 9 oz) jap (kent) pumpkin, peeled
2 tablespoons olive oil
grated zest and juice of 1 lime
1 tablespoon fish sauce
1 tablespoon soy sauce
100 ml (3½ fl oz) mirin
2 bunches broccolini (about 400 g/14 oz in total),
    trimmed
200 g (7 oz) firm tofu, cut into 2 cm (¾ inch) cubes
1 tablespoon sesame seeds, toasted

Preheat the oven to 180°C (350°F/Gas 4). Cut the pumpkin into bite-sized pieces and put them in a large bowl. Add the olive oil and season with sea salt and freshly ground black pepper. Toss until the pumpkin is well coated, then transfer to a baking tray and roast for 20 minutes, or until golden brown and tender.

Put the lime zest, lime juice, fish sauce, soy sauce and mirin in a large non-metallic bowl and stir to make a dressing.

Bring a saucepan of water to the boil. Add the broccolini and blanch for 2 minutes, or until just tender. Drain the broccolini, then add to the dressing along with the pumpkin, tofu and sesame seeds. Gently toss to mix the dressing through. Serves 4–6

Opposite: lamb skewers with herbed yoghurt
Over: fried shallot and cashew salad; roast pumpkin and tofu salad

salmon wrapped in vine leaves

4 x 150 g (5$^{1}/_{2}$ oz) salmon fillets, bones and
    skin removed
16 preserved vine leaves
250 g (9 oz) cherry tomatoes
185 g (6$^{1}/_{2}$ oz/1 cup) instant couscous
1 tablespoon butter
1 handful flat-leaf (Italian) parsley, roughly chopped
2 spring onions (scallions), finely sliced
olive oil, for drizzling
lemon wedges, to serve

Preheat the oven to 200°C (400°F/Gas 6). Rinse the salmon under running water and pat dry with paper towels. Rinse the vine leaves several times to remove some of the saltiness, but leave them slightly wet to make them easier to work with.

Lay four vine leaves on a clean surface with their edges generously overlapping. Lay a salmon fillet in the middle, then wrap the leaves around the fish. Repeat with the remaining vine leaves and salmon fillets to make four parcels. Put them on a baking tray with the whole cherry tomatoes and bake for 15 minutes.

Meanwhile, put the couscous and butter in a large bowl and pour 250 ml (9 fl oz/1 cup) of boiling water over the top. Cover and allow to sit for 5 minutes, then fluff up the grains with a fork. Cover again and leave for a further 5 minutes. When the couscous has absorbed all the water, rub the grains with your fingertips to remove any lumps.

Remove the salmon from the oven. Add the roasted cherry tomatoes to the couscous along with the parsley and spring onion. Lightly toss together. Divide the salmon parcels among four plates and peel the vine leaves open. Spoon the couscous over the middle of the salmon and serve with a drizzle of olive oil and lemon wedges. Serves 4

chicken and pine nut salad

1 tablespoon sea salt
2 boneless, skinless chicken breasts
1 egg yolk
zest and juice of 1 lemon
125 ml (4 fl oz/$^{1}/_{2}$ cup) light olive oil
2 anchovy fillets, finely chopped
3 tablespoons small salted capers, rinsed
    and drained
3 tablespoons pine nuts, toasted
3 tablespoons currants
1 very large handful flat-leaf (Italian) parsley,
    roughly chopped
warm crusty bread, to serve

Put a large pot of water over high heat, add the sea salt and bring to the boil. Add the chicken breasts, then cover the pot and take it off the heat for 40 minutes — during this time the residual heat will gently poach the chicken. Lift the chicken out of the water and allow to cool before shredding the meat.

In a small bowl, whisk together the egg yolk and lemon juice. Slowly add the olive oil, whisking continually to form a thick, creamy mayonnaise. Fold the anchovies through and season with salt and freshly ground black pepper.

Toss the shredded chicken in a large bowl with the lemon zest, capers, pine nuts, currants and parsley. Mix the anchovy mayonnaise through the salad, then spoon into four bowls and serve with warm crusty bread. Serves 4

wrap fresh fish in salty, aromatic vine leaves

Opposite: salmon wrapped in vine leaves
Over: chicken and pine nut salad

lentil and beetroot salad

4 beetroot (beets) (about 150 g/5^1/$_2$ oz each),
    washed but not peeled
100 g (3^1/$_2$ oz/^{1}/$_2$ cup) puy lentils or tiny
    blue-green lentils
^{1}/$_2$ teaspoon sea salt
1 teaspoon balsamic vinegar
1 tablespoon extra virgin olive oil
juice of 1 orange
100 g (3^1/$_2$ oz/2^1/$_3$ cups) baby rocket (arugula) leaves
100 g (3^1/$_2$ oz) marinated goat's cheese

Preheat the oven to 200°C (400°F/Gas 6). Sit the
beetroot in a roasting tin and pour in 250 ml (9 fl oz/
1 cup) of water. Cover with foil and bake for 1 hour,
or until a knife passes easily through the beetroot.
Remove the beetroot from the tin and leave to cool.

Meanwhile, put the lentils in a saucepan with 500 ml
(17 fl oz/2 cups) of water. Add the sea salt and bring
to the boil, then reduce the heat and simmer for
20–30 minutes, or until the lentils are tender. Drain
off any excess water, tip the lentils into a bowl and
stir in the vinegar and olive oil.

Wearing rubber gloves to stop your hands staining,
peel the skins from the beetroot — they should slip
free quite easily. Cut the bulbs into wedges, put them
in a bowl and pour the orange juice over the top.

Scatter the rocket leaves on a serving platter and
arrange the beetroot wedges on top. Spoon the lentils
over the top, season with a little sea salt and freshly
ground black pepper and drizzle with any remaining
orange and beetroot juice. Crumble the goat's cheese
over the top. Serves 4

lentil and beetroot salad

chilli beef salad

1 tablespoon grated fresh ginger
2 garlic cloves, crushed
1 teaspoon ground turmeric
1 teaspoon sea salt
4 tablespoons olive oil
800 g (1 lb 12 oz) piece of scotch or rib fillet
1 red onion, finely sliced
1 ripe tomato, finely chopped
1/2 teaspoon garam masala
1 large red chilli, seeded and sliced lengthways
125 ml (4 1/2 fl oz/1/2 cup) shaoxing rice wine
100 g (3 1/2 oz/2 3/4 cups) mixed salad leaves

Put the ginger, garlic, turmeric, sea salt and olive oil
in a small bowl. Mix to a paste, then rub the paste
all over the beef.

Heat a large, heavy-based frying pan over medium
heat. Sear the beef for 5 minutes on one side, then
turn and sear the other side for 5 minutes. Lift the
beef onto a plate, cover with foil and allow to rest.

Using the same frying pan, cook the onion, tomato,
garam masala and chilli in the pan juices for 2 minutes,
stirring constantly. Stir in the rice wine and 125 ml
(4 fl oz/1/2 cup) of water and simmer for 5 minutes,
or until thickened slightly.

Divide the salad leaves among four bowls. Finely slice
the beef and arrange the slices over the top. Serve each
salad topped with several spoonfuls of the onion and
tomato mixture, drizzled with the pan juices. Serves 4

pumpkin and hazelnut salad

1 kg (2 lb 4 oz) jap (kent) pumpkin
1 tablespoon vegetable oil
100 g (3 1/2 oz/3/4 cup) hazelnuts
3 tablespoons tahini
125 g (4 1/2 oz/1/2 cup) plain yoghurt
1 teaspoon ground cumin
1/2 teaspoon finely chopped garlic
1 tablespoon lemon juice
200 g (7 oz/2 small bunches) rocket (arugula),
    stalks removed
1 tablespoon olive oil
1 teaspoon red wine vinegar

Preheat the oven to 180°C (350°F/Gas 4). Peel the
pumpkin and cut it into bite-sized chunks. Toss them
in a bowl with the vegetable oil and season with
sea salt and freshly ground black pepper. Spread the
pumpkin on a baking tray and roast for 20 minutes,
or until golden brown. Meanwhile, roast the hazelnuts
on another baking tray for 5 minutes, or until the skins
start splitting. Remove and allow to cool.

Mix the tahini, yoghurt, cumin, garlic and lemon juice
to a smooth paste, then season to taste.

Rub the skins off the cooled hazelnuts and roughly
chop the nuts. Put them in a bowl with the rocket
and add the olive oil and vinegar. Toss together, then
divide the leaves among four plates. Top with the
pumpkin chunks and dollop with the tahini mixture.
Serves 4

a richly flavoured collision of indian spices and juicy beef

Opposite: chilli beef salad
Over: pumpkin and hazelnut salad

sesame greens

Trim 350 g (12 oz/2 bunches) asparagus spears, then slice each one in half down along its length. Trim 200 g (7 oz) snow peas (mangetout), and cut 2 baby bok choy (pak choy) into quarters. Dissolve 1 teaspoon cornflour (cornstarch) in 125 ml (4 fl oz/^{1}/$_2$ cup) water and pour the mixture into a wok or heavy-based saucepan. Stir in 3^1/$_2$ tablespoons oyster sauce, 1^1/$_2$ tablespoons mirin and 1 teaspoon sugar. Put the wok over high heat and, when the sauce begins to bubble, add the green vegetables and 1 tablespoon sesame seeds and toss for 2–3 minutes, or until the vegetables are just tender and cooked through. Drizzle with 1 tablespoon lime juice, toss again, then pile onto a serving platter. Serves 4

rocket and pear salad

Trim the stalks from 200 g (7 oz/2 small bunches) rocket (arugula) and put the leaves in a salad bowl with 2 thinly sliced beurre bosc pears and 100 g (3^1/$_2$ oz/1^1/$_2$ cups) shaved parmesan cheese. In a small bowl, mix together 1 teaspoon white wine vinegar, 1 teaspoon dijon mustard and ^{1}/$_2$ teaspoon honey. Slowly whisk in 2 tablespoons olive oil, then season with sea salt and freshly ground black pepper and drizzle over the salad. Serves 4

tofu, broccolini and almonds

Cut 300 g (10½ oz) silken tofu into 2 cm (¾ inch) cubes and put them in a large bowl. Slice 3 seeded large red chillies into fine, long strips. Cut 235 g (8½ oz/1 bunch) broccolini in half, then cut the thicker pieces in half along the stalk. Heat 2 tablespoons olive oil in a wok over high heat. Add 2 teaspoons finely grated fresh ginger and 2 crushed garlic cloves. As soon as they start to sizzle, add 2 tablespoons soy sauce and 2 tablespoons mirin. When the sauce begins to bubble, add the broccolini and stir-fry for 2 minutes. Add the chilli strips and stir-fry for 1 minute, then scoop the vegetables over the tofu, leaving the sauce in the wok. Add 1 tablespoon butter to the wok, then 50 g (1¾ oz/ heaped ½ cup) flaked almonds. Stir for 30 seconds, or until the sauce thickly coats the almonds, then spoon the almonds over the vegetables. Serves 4

avocado and sumac salad

In a bowl, whisk together 4 tablespoons extra virgin olive oil, 1 tablespoon white wine vinegar, ½ teaspoon honey, 1 teaspoon dijon mustard and 2 teaspoons sumac to make a dressing. Peel 1 telegraph (long) cucumber, slice it in half lengthways and scoop out the seeds with a teaspoon. Slice the cucumber thickly on the diagonal, then put it in a large bowl with 4 small, quartered, ripe tomatoes, 1 diced avocado and 3 tablespoons oregano leaves. Remove the dark outer leaves from 1 cos (romaine) lettuce, slice the heart into thick strips and gently toss them through the salad along with the sumac dressing. Transfer to a serving bowl and sprinkle lightly with a little extra sumac. Serves 4–6

sea

summer sands   clear blue waters

swimmers and fins   salt and spice

Island food, health food, easy food, seafood. For sheer simplicity and flavour, freshly caught seafood is the perfect ingredient. It's quick to cook and is just as wonderful with a scatter of salt and a squeeze of lime as it is with a marinade of Indian spices or a tangy Asian sauce. For those of us lucky enough to live beside the too-blue sea, it is also the obvious choice. And for the city-bound, who can resist a trip to the fish markets: all those pearly scales and shimmering tails lying on beds of ice — big fish, little fish, mounds of seaside shells and skittering crabs.

116

steamed fish with watercress salad

4 x 150 g (5½ oz) blue-eye cod fillets
1 telegraph (long) cucumber, peeled, seeded
    and finely julienned
2 large handfuls watercress sprigs
2 tablespoons fish sauce
2 tablespoons lime juice
1½ tablespoons white wine vinegar
1 tablespoon grated fresh ginger
1 teaspoon sugar
1 large red chilli, seeded and finely chopped
steamed white rice (Basics), to serve

Fill a large, wide pot with 6 cm (2½ inches) of water
and bring it to the boil.

Rest the base of a bamboo steamer in the boiling
water. Line a second bamboo basket with a large
square of baking paper, sit the fish fillets on the paper
and season with a little sea salt. Cover the basket,
then sit it on top of the bamboo steamer and allow
the fish to steam for 7–8 minutes, depending on the
thickness of the fillets.

Meanwhile, toss the cucumber and watercress in a
large bowl. In a small bowl mix together the fish sauce,
lime juice, vinegar, ginger, sugar and chilli to make a
dressing. Stir until the sugar has dissolved, then pour
the dressing over the watercress and lightly toss.

Remove the cooked fish from the steamer and
arrange on four warmed plates. Top with the salad,
drizzle with any remaining dressing and serve with
steamed white rice. Serves 4

chargrilled prawns with lime aïoli

1 large green chilli, seeded
1 garlic clove
1 teaspoon dried oregano
½ teaspoon ground cumin
grated zest and juice of 1 lime
juice of 1 orange
4 tablespoons olive oil
24 large raw prawns (shrimp), peeled and
    deveined, tails intact

lime aïoli
4 garlic cloves
½ teaspoon salt
1 egg yolk
½ teaspoon finely grated lime zest
2 teaspoons lime juice
170 ml (5½ fl oz/⅔ cup) olive oil

Using a mortar and pestle or small blender, grind
the chilli, garlic, oregano, cumin, lime zest, lime juice,
orange juice and olive oil together to make a marinade.
Season with a little sea salt and ground white pepper.
Toss the prawns in the marinade, then cover and
refrigerate for 1 hour.

Meanwhile, soak 24 small bamboo skewers in cold
water for 30 minutes to prevent scorching.

To make the lime aïoli, pound the garlic and salt to a
smooth paste using a mortar and pestle. Scrape the
paste into a large bowl, then whisk in the egg yolk,
lime zest and lime juice. Whisking continually, slowly
add the olive oil a little at a time, until you have a thick
mayonnaise. Season to taste, then cover and refrigerate
until ready to use. Makes about 160 g (5¾ oz/⅔ cup).

Heat a barbecue flat plate, chargrill or grill (broiler) to
high. Drain the skewers and thread a prawn onto each
one. Cook the prawns for 1½ minutes, or until they
just turn pink and start to curl, then turn and cook for
a further 1½ minutes, or until just opaque. Serve at
once with the lime aïoli. Serves 4

tantalizingly healthy with a touch of chilli and ginger

Opposite: steamed fish with watercress salad
Over: chargrilled prawns with lime aïoli

mussel and squid salad

1 kg (2 lb 4 oz) black mussels
20 small squid (about 2 kg/4 lb 8 oz in total),
    cleaned, tentacles removed
3 tablespoons olive oil
250 ml (9 fl oz/1 cup) dry white wine
4 tablespoons white wine vinegar
3 thyme sprigs
zest and juice of 2 lemons
4 ripe roma (plum) tomatoes, roughly chopped
2 garlic cloves, crushed
4 spring onions (scallions), finely sliced
3 tablespoons roughly chopped parsley
olive oil, extra, for drizzling
baby salad leaves, to serve

Clean the mussels under cold running water, scrubbing them to remove any barnacles or bits of hairy 'beard'. Throw away any broken ones, or any open ones that don't close when you tap them. Slice the squid into 2 cm (3/4 inch) strips.

Put the olive oil, wine, vinegar and thyme sprigs in a saucepan. Bring to the boil, then reduce to a simmer over low heat. Add the mussels, then cover the pan and cook for 1 1/2–2 minutes, shaking the pan now and then. Using a slotted spoon, remove the mussels as they open and throw away any that remain closed.

Add the squid to the simmering liquid and cook for 2–3 minutes, or until soft and cooked through. Drain the squid, discarding the liquid, and place in a large bowl. Pull the mussels out of their shells and add them to the squid, along with the lemon zest, lemon juice, tomato, garlic, spring onion and parsley. Toss together, then cover and refrigerate for 1 hour. Season with sea salt and freshly ground black pepper and serve with a drizzle of olive oil on a bed of baby salad leaves. Serves 4

spicy prawn salad

20 cooked prawns (shrimp), peeled and deveined
1 large red chilli, seeded and finely chopped
1/2 teaspoon cayenne pepper
1/2 teaspoon ground cumin
1 tablespoon finely grated fresh ginger
2 spring onions (scallions), finely sliced
2 tablespoons lime juice
4 tablespoons olive oil
1 handful coriander (cilantro) leaves
2 small avocados, diced
steamed couscous (Basics), to serve

Put the prawns in a bowl with the chilli, cayenne pepper, cumin, ginger, spring onion, lime juice and olive oil.

Toss to coat the prawns well, then add the coriander and avocado and season to taste. Lightly toss again and serve on a bed of steamed couscous. Serves 4

a chilled seafood salad for hot days by the sea

Opposite: mussel and squid salad
Over: spicy prawn salad

squid and fennel salad

squid and fennel salad

8 small squid (about 750 g/1 lb 10 oz in total),
    cleaned (reserve the tentacles)
2 garlic cloves, crushed
1/2 teaspoon ground white pepper
3 tablespoons olive oil
3 tablespoons lemon juice
2 fennel bulbs
16 kalamata olives, pitted and roughly chopped
1 handful parsley, roughly chopped
1 tablespoon finely chopped mint
3 tablespoons unsalted butter

Rinse the squid under cold running water and pat dry with paper towels. Cut the tubes along one side and open them out into a flat piece. Using a sharp knife, lightly score the inside surface with crisscross lines — don't cut too deeply, just enough to mark the flesh. Slice into 3 cm (1 1/4 inch) wide strips and put the strips and tentacles in a non-metallic bowl. Add the garlic, white pepper, olive oil and lemon juice, then toss well to coat. Cover and refrigerate for 1 hour.

Very finely slice the fennel and place in a bowl with the olives, parsley and mint. Season lightly with sea salt and freshly ground black pepper.

Drain the squid, reserving the marinating liquid. Heat 1 tablespoon of the butter in a non-stick frying pan over medium heat and add the squid a few pieces at a time. Cook for 2 1/2 minutes on each side, or until the flesh is opaque, then add the squid to the fennel. Cook the remaining squid in two more batches, adding more butter as needed.

When all the squid is cooked, add the marinating liquid and any remaining butter to the pan and simmer over medium heat until the butter has melted. Pour the pan juices over the salad and toss well. Serves 4

tangy shellfish broth

8 raw king prawns (shrimp)
3 lemon grass stems
100 g (3¹/2 oz) oyster mushrooms, cut in half
100 g (3¹/2 oz) enoki mushrooms
6 makrut (kaffir lime) leaves
3 roma (plum) tomatoes, finely chopped
2 spring onions (scallions), finely sliced
juice of 3 limes
1 large red chilli, seeded and finely chopped
2–4 tablespoons fish sauce, or to taste
50 g (1³/4 oz/¹/2 cup) fresh crabmeat
1 handful coriander (cilantro), roughly chopped
1 handful mint

Peel and devein the prawns, reserving the shells.
Slice off and reserve the white ends of the lemon
grass stems, then cut the long green stalks into 2 cm
(³/4 inch) lengths and flatten them with a cleaver or
the end of a heavy-handled knife.

Heat 1 litre (35 fl oz/4 cups) of water in a saucepan.
Add the prawn shells and the white ends of the lemon
grass and bring to the boil. Once the water has come
to the boil, take the pan off the heat and strain the
prawn stock into a large bowl to remove the solids.

Pour the prawn stock back into the saucepan, then
add the crushed green lemon grass stalks, mushrooms,
lime leaves and tomato. Return to the boil, then reduce
the heat and simmer for 3–4 minutes. Add the prawns,
and when they start to turn pink, add the spring onion,
lime juice, chilli, fish sauce and crabmeat. Stir well,
then season to taste. Ladle into warmed bowls and
serve with a sprinkle of coriander and mint. Serves 4
as a starter, or 2 as a main

black bean scallops

1 tablespoon finely grated fresh ginger
25 g (1 oz/1 bunch) chives, finely snipped
2 tablespoons Chinese salted black beans
¹/2 teaspoon sesame oil
4 tablespoons dry sherry
2 tablespoons lemon juice
100 g (3¹/2 oz/2¹/4 cups) baby English spinach leaves
750 g (1 lb 10 oz) scallops, with roe
2¹/2 tablespoons butter
lemon wedges, to serve

Put the ginger, chives, black beans, sesame oil, sherry
and lemon juice in a bowl and stir lightly to combine.
Divide the spinach leaves among four plates.

Remove the membrane and any vein or tough white
muscle from the scallops, leaving the roe attached.
Rinse well and pat dry with paper towels.

Melt 2 teaspoons of the butter in a large, heavy-based
frying pan over high heat. When the butter begins to
froth, add the scallops in several batches and sear for
30 seconds on each side, adding the remaining butter
as needed. Remove the scallops with a slotted spoon
and gently scatter them over the spinach leaves.

Put the frying pan back over high heat. When the pan
juices begin to bubble, add the black bean mixture
and quickly swirl around the pan for a minute to warm
through. Spoon the sauce over the scallops and serve
with lemon wedges. Serves 4

limes and lemon grass, prawns and crabmeat

tangy shellfish broth

black bean scallops

mussels in tamarind broth

2 kg (4 lb 8 oz) mussels
2 tablespoons vegetable oil
1 teaspoon ground coriander
1/2 teaspoon ground turmeric
1 clove
1 teaspoon finely grated fresh ginger
1 large red chilli, seeded and finely chopped
2 garlic cloves, finely chopped
4 spring onions (scallions), finely sliced
2 tablespoons tamarind purée
150 ml (5 fl oz) coconut milk
juice of 1 lime
1 handful coriander (cilantro) sprigs
steamed coconut rice (Basics), to serve (optional)

Clean the mussels under cold running water, scrubbing them to remove any barnacles or bits of hairy 'beard'. Throw away any broken ones, or any open ones that don't close when you tap them.

Heat the oil in a large saucepan over medium heat. Add the ground coriander, turmeric and clove, then stir in the ginger and chilli. Add the garlic and spring onion and cook for 1 minute, stirring, then add the tamarind purée and 125 ml (4 fl oz/1/2 cup) of water and bring to the boil.

Add the mussels, then cover and cook for 2 minutes, or until all the mussels have opened, then take the pan off the heat. Scoop the mussels out with a slotted spoon, leaving the tamarind broth in the pan. Throw away any mussels that haven't opened and divide the rest among four serving bowls.

Put the pan back over medium heat and stir in the coconut milk and lime juice. Simmer for 1 minute, then spoon the broth over the mussels and scatter with the coriander sprigs. Serve as is, or for a more substantial meal, serve with side bowls of steamed coconut rice. Serves 4

squid with red capsicum sauce

10 small squid (about 1 kg/2 lb 4 oz in total),
   cleaned (reserve the tentacles)
1/4 teaspoon chilli flakes
140 ml (41/2 fl oz) olive oil
1 garlic clove, roughly chopped
1 tablespoon finely chopped oregano
3 roasted red capsicums (peppers), seeds,
   membranes and skin removed (Basics)
2 tablespoons lemon juice
100 g (31/2 oz/23/4 cups) rocket (arugula) leaves
2 Lebanese (short) cucumbers, roughly chopped
2 tablespoons extra virgin olive oil
lemon wedges, to serve

Rinse the squid under cold running water and pat dry with paper towels. Cut the tubes along one side and open them out into a flat piece. Using a sharp knife, lightly score the inside surface with crisscross lines to make the squid curl up during cooking — don't cut too deeply, just enough to mark the flesh. Slice into 3 cm (1 1/4 inch) wide strips and put the strips and tentacles in a non-metallic bowl. Add the chilli flakes and 3 tablespoons of the olive oil, then toss well to coat the squid. Cover and chill for 1–2 hours.

To make the red capsicum sauce, put the remaining olive oil in a food processor with the garlic, oregano, capsicum and 1 tablespoon of the lemon juice. Add a good pinch of sea salt and blend into a sauce. Set aside.

Put the remaining lemon juice in a bowl with the rocket, cucumber and extra virgin olive oil. Season with sea salt and freshly ground black pepper and toss well. Spoon the sauce onto four serving plates, smoothing it into a pool. Top with the rocket salad.

Working in batches, cook the squid on a hot barbecue grill plate or chargrill pan for 1–2 minutes on each side, or until it turns opaque and sears brown in a few places. Pile the squid on top of the salad and serve with lemon wedges. Serves 4

aromatic mussels in a sweet and sour broth

Opposite: mussels in tamarind broth
Over: squid with red capsicum sauce

pickled swordfish salad

4 tablespoons olive oil

2 red onions, thinly sliced

2 green chillies, seeded and finely sliced

2 garlic cloves, finely chopped

1 teaspoon ground cumin

2 tablespoons finely chopped lemon grass,
 white part only

500 g (1 lb 2 oz) cherry tomatoes, cut in half,
 or into quarters if large

600 g (1 lb 5 oz) swordfish, cut into 1.5 cm
 (5/8 inch) cubes

1 handful coriander (cilantro) leaves

15 mint leaves, roughly torn

250 ml (9 fl oz/1 cup) lemon juice

baby leaf salad, to serve

Heat the olive oil in a heavy-based frying pan over
medium heat and add the onion, chilli, garlic, cumin
and lemon grass. Cook, stirring, for 5 minutes, or until
the onion is translucent, then add the cherry tomatoes
and cook for 1 minute, or until they are just starting
to soften. Take the pan off the heat and allow the
tomato mixture to cool completely.

Arrange the raw fish in a single layer in a wide,
non-metallic dish. Spread the tomato mixture over the
top, then sprinkle with the coriander and mint. Pour
the lemon juice over the top, then cover and marinate
overnight in the refrigerator. Bring to room temperature
and serve with a baby leaf salad. Serves 4

pickled swordfish salad

pan-fried bream with parsley salad

1 large handful flat-leaf (Italian) parsley, chopped
250 g (9 oz) cherry tomatoes, cut in half
25 g (1 oz/1 bunch) chives, snipped into 3 cm
    (1¼ inch) lengths
½ red onion, finely sliced
2 tablespoons small salted capers, rinsed and drained
zest and juice of 1 lemon
2 tablespoons olive oil
100 g (3½ oz/scant 1 cup) fine semolina
1 tablespoon finely chopped dill
4 x 150 g (5½ oz) bream fillets
2½ tablespoons butter
lemon wedges, to serve

Preheat the oven to 180°C (350°F/Gas 4). To make the parsley salad, put the parsley, cherry tomatoes, chives, onion, capers, lemon zest, lemon juice and olive oil in a bowl and toss well. Season with freshly ground black pepper and set aside.

Put the semolina and dill in a bowl and mix together well. Season with sea salt and freshly ground black pepper.

Rinse the bream under cold running water and pat dry with paper towels. Dip each fish fillet in the semolina mixture and gently press to coat well on both sides.

Heat the butter in a large frying pan over medium heat and fry the bream fillets for 2 minutes on each side, or until lightly golden. Now put them on a baking tray lined with foil and bake for 5 minutes, or until cooked through. Serve with the parsley salad and lemon wedges. Serves 4

coconut simmered fish

2 lemon grass stems
4 makrut (kaffir lime) leaves
4 spring onions (scallions), trimmed and cut into
    3 cm (1¼ inch) lengths
200 ml (7 fl oz) coconut milk
2 large red chillies, halved lengthways and seeded
1 garlic clove, finely chopped
1 tablespoon finely grated fresh ginger
4 x 150 g (5½ oz) blue-eye cod fillets
1 teaspoon fish sauce
steamed white rice (Basics), to serve
coriander (cilantro) sprigs, to serve

Trim the lemon grass stems, then cut the stalks in half across the middle and flatten them with a cleaver or the end of a heavy-handled knife. Put them in a wide-based saucepan with the lime leaves, spring onion, coconut milk, chilli halves, garlic and ginger. Add 125 ml (4 fl oz/½ cup) of water and simmer over low heat for 5 minutes.

Rinse the fish fillets under cold running water and pat dry with paper towels. Sprinkle lightly with sea salt, then sit them in the simmering coconut milk in a single layer. Cover and simmer for 8 minutes, or until the fish is cooked through.

Lift the fillets out with a spatula and stir the fish sauce into the coconut milk. Serve the fish on a bed of steamed white rice with generous spoonfuls of the sauce, scattered with coriander sprigs and the red chilli halves. Serves 4

ocean trout with cucumber salad

1 teaspoon ground cumin
½ teaspoon ground coriander
½ teaspoon dried oregano
½ teaspoon ground turmeric
¼ teaspoon cayenne pepper
1 garlic clove, finely chopped
finely grated zest and juice of 2 limes
4 x 150 g (5½ oz) ocean trout fillets
3 Lebanese (short) cucumbers
10 mint leaves, finely chopped
1 tablespoon extra virgin olive oil
4 lime wedges

In a non-metallic bowl, mix together the cumin, coriander, oregano, turmeric, cayenne pepper, garlic, lime zest and lime juice. Add the trout fillets, and turn them about to coat all over. Cover and marinate in the refrigerator for 1 hour.

Preheat the oven to 180°C (350°F/Gas 4). To make the cucumber salad, finely slice the cucumbers and put them in a bowl with the mint, olive oil and a sprinkle of sea salt. Set aside.

Sit the trout fillets on a baking tray lined with foil, season with a little sea salt and bake for 10 minutes, or until the flesh flakes when tested with a fork — it should still be a little rare in the middle. Serve with the cucumber salad and a wedge of lime. Serves 4

Opposite: pan-fried bream with parsley salad

coconut simmered fish

ocean trout with cucumber salad

prawn and chicken salad

350 g (12 oz) small cooked prawns (shrimp)
1 teaspoon ground cumin
2 teaspoons fish sauce
4 tablespoons lime juice
4 tablespoons olive oil
1 tablespoon sesame oil
15 mint leaves, finely sliced
1 teaspoon sugar
2 cooked boneless, skinless chicken breasts, shredded
1 carrot, grated
100 g (3 1/2 oz) snow pea (mangetout) sprouts
1 telegraph (long) cucumber, peeled, seeded and diced
2 spring onions (scallions), finely sliced
1 baby cos (romaine) lettuce, finely sliced
1–2 tablespoons sesame seeds, toasted

Peel the prawns and put them in a large bowl.

In a small bowl, combine the cumin, fish sauce, lime juice, olive oil, sesame oil, mint and sugar. Stir until the sugar has dissolved, then pour the mixture over the prawns and toss until the prawns are well coated.

Add the chicken, carrot, snow pea sprouts, cucumber, spring onion and lettuce. Lightly toss together, then pile onto a serving platter or into individual bowls and sprinkle with the sesame seeds. Serves 4–6

seared swordfish with black-eyed peas

200 g (7 oz/1 cup) black-eyed peas
3 handfuls flat-leaf (Italian) parsley, roughly chopped
1/4 red onion, finely diced
15 mint leaves, finely chopped
3 tablespoons extra virgin olive oil
juice of 1 lemon
1 teaspoon white wine vinegar
1 tablespoon olive oil
4 × 180 g (6 oz) swordfish steaks
2 lemons, cut into wedges

Soak the black-eyed peas in plenty of cold water for 6–8 hours, or overnight. Drain and rinse well, then put them in a saucepan with plenty of water. Simmer over low heat, uncovered, for 45–60 minutes, or until tender — the actual cooking time will depend on how fresh they are. Drain, rinse well and leave to cool.

Toss the black-eyed peas in a bowl with the parsley, onion, mint, extra virgin olive oil, lemon juice and vinegar. Season generously with sea salt and freshly ground black pepper.

Heat the olive oil in a large heavy-based frying pan over high heat and fry the swordfish steaks for 2–3 minutes on each side, or until cooked through. Serve with lemon wedges and the black-eyed pea salad. Serves 4

a hammock, a fork and a bowl of sunshine

Opposite: prawn and chicken salad

seared swordfish with black-eyed peas

salmon carpaccio

Take a 300 g (10½ oz) piece of sashimi-quality salmon, remove any small bones, then wrap it in plastic wrap and freeze for 1 hour. Meanwhile, in a non-metallic bowl, toss together 2 small, very finely sliced Lebanese (short) cucumbers, ½ teaspoon sea salt, 1 teaspoon finely chopped mint, 1 teaspoon finely chopped dill, 1 teaspoon sugar and the juice of 1 lemon. Cover and refrigerate for 1 hour. Using a very sharp knife, cut the chilled fish into thin slices. Divide among four small plates and spoon the cucumber salad over the top, reserving any liquid left in the bowl. In a small bowl, combine 2 tablespoons sour cream and 1 teaspoon grated fresh horseradish or horseradish cream. Stir in enough reserved cucumber liquid to make a thin dressing, then drizzle over the cucumber and salmon. Serve garnished with a dill sprig. Serves 4

white fish carpaccio with asian salsa

Take a 250 g (9 oz) piece of sashimi-quality trevally, snapper or pomfret and remove any bones. Wrap it in plastic wrap and freeze for 1 hour. Meanwhile, make the salsa. In a bowl, toss together 1 finely diced Lebanese (short) cucumber, 1 seeded and finely diced large red chilli, ½ finely diced yellow capsicum (pepper), 1 finely sliced spring onion (scallion), 1 tablespoon finely chopped coriander (cilantro), 1 teaspoon finely chopped lemon grass (white part only) and 1 teaspoon finely grated fresh ginger. In another bowl put 2 tablespoons lime juice, 1 tablespoon fish sauce, 1 teaspoon sugar and 1 teaspoon sesame oil. Stir until the sugar has dissolved, then pour the dressing over the salsa and gently mix. Using a very sharp knife, cut the chilled fish into paper-thin slices. Divide among four small plates and spoon the salsa over the top. Serves 4

sweet pickled ocean trout

Take a 300 g (10½ oz) piece of fresh ocean trout and remove any bones and skin. Wrap it in plastic wrap and freeze for 1 hour. Put 1 tablespoon grated fresh ginger in a non-metallic bowl with the juice of 4 limes, 10 finely chopped mint leaves, 1 tablespoon soy sauce and 1 tablespoon sesame oil. Add 1 tablespoon finely chopped Japanese pickled ginger, and 4 tablespoons pickling liquid from the pickled ginger. Mix well. Using a very sharp knife, cut the chilled fish into thin slices, put them in a non-metallic dish and add the ginger mixture. Cover and refrigerate for 1 hour. Divide 100 g (3½ oz/2¼ cups) baby English spinach leaves among four small bowls and scatter with 3–4 tablespoons freshly grated daikon. Top with the pickled salmon, sprinkle with black sesame seeds and drizzle with the pickled ginger juices. Serves 4

herbed ceviche with avocado salad

Take a 250 g (9 oz) fillet of very fresh bream, wrap it in plastic wrap and freeze for 1 hour. In a non-metallic bowl, mix together the juice of 2 limes, ½ teaspoon sesame oil, 2 teaspoons grated palm sugar or soft brown sugar, 2 teaspoons soy sauce, 4 tablespoons coconut milk, 1 tablespoon finely chopped mint and 1 tablespoon finely chopped coriander (cilantro). Using a sharp knife, cut the fish into paper-thin slices and add them to the marinade. Cover and refrigerate for 1 hour. Put 1 finely diced avocado in a small bowl, drizzle with 1½ tablespoons olive oil and lightly stir to coat. To serve, arrange the fish on four small plates and pile a mound of avocado in the middle of each. Drizzle with a little of the marinade and season with freshly ground black pepper. Serves 4

sweet and sour prawns

1/2 teaspoon cayenne pepper
1 teaspoon ground turmeric
1 tablespoon tamarind purée
20 raw king prawns (shrimp), peeled and deveined,
    tails intact
2 tablespoons vegetable oil
2 red onions, finely sliced
1 red capsicum (pepper), cut into 1 cm (1/2 inch) cubes
1 tablespoon grated palm sugar or soft brown sugar
1 tablespoon balsamic vinegar
100 ml (3 1/2 fl oz) coconut milk
1 handful coriander (cilantro) sprigs
steamed white rice (Basics), to serve

Put the cayenne pepper, turmeric and tamarind purée
in a non-metallic bowl and stir to combine. Add the
prawns and toss until well coated. Cover and
refrigerate until ready to cook.

Put the oil in a large heavy-based frying pan over
medium–low heat. Add the onion and cook for
20 minutes, stirring occasionally, until the onion is
soft and beginning to caramelize. Add the capsicum,
sugar and vinegar and cook for a further 2 minutes.

Add the prawns, laying them on their sides in a single
layer over the onion mixture, and cook for 1 1/2–2 minutes
on each side, or until they are starting to curl up and
turn pink — you may need to cook the prawns in two
batches if your pan isn't quite large enough to fit them
all at once. Serve the prawns and sauce over steamed
white rice, drizzled with the coconut milk and
scattered with the coriander sprigs. Serves 4

banana leaf fish

2 tablespoons vegetable oil
1 onion, diced
60 g (2 1/4 oz/2/3 cup) desiccated coconut
1/4 teaspoon chilli powder
1/4 teaspoon ground turmeric
1 tablespoon wholegrain mustard
4 squares of banana leaf or baking paper, each
    measuring 25 x 25 cm (10 x 10 inches)
4 x 150 g (5 1/2 oz) blue-eye cod fillets
lime wedges, to serve
steamed white rice (Basics), to serve

Preheat the oven to 180°C (350°F/Gas 4). Heat the oil
in a non-stick frying pan over medium–low heat. Add
the onion and cook for 5 minutes, or until soft and
translucent, then add the coconut, chilli powder and
turmeric. Increase the heat to medium and cook,
stirring, for 2–3 minutes, or until the coconut is golden
brown. Transfer to a small food processor or blender
and blend to a smooth paste. Scrape the coconut
paste into a small bowl and stir the mustard through.

If using banana leaves, run them quickly over a hot
gas flame to soften the leaves, or quickly blanch them
in a pot of boiling water for 30 seconds.

Place a square of banana leaf or baking paper on
a clean surface and top with a piece of fish. Season
the fish with a little sea salt, then spread 2 heaped
tablespoons of the coconut paste over the top. Wrap
up the parcel firmly and sit it on a baking tray. Repeat
with the remaining ingredients to make four parcels.
Bake for 25 minutes, or until the fish is cooked
through. Serve with lime wedges and steamed
white rice. Serves 4

coconut snapper

4 small snapper (about 400 g/14 oz each)
4 spring onions (scallions), finely sliced
2 garlic cloves, finely chopped
1 tablespoon finely grated fresh ginger
2 large red chillies, seeded and finely chopped
300 ml (10 1/2 fl oz) tin coconut milk
steamed white rice (Basics), to serve
stir-fried Chinese greens, to serve

Using a sharp knife, make several 5 mm (1/4 inch)
deep cuts into the thickest part of each snapper, on
both sides of the fish. In a small bowl, mix together
the spring onion, garlic, ginger, chilli and coconut milk.
Sit the fish in a single layer in a large baking dish and
pour the coconut milk mixture over the top. Cover
with foil and marinate in the refrigerator for 2 hours.

Preheat the oven to 180°C (350°F/Gas 4). Put the
foil-covered dish in the oven and bake the fish for
20 minutes, or until cooked through. Lift the fish out
with a spatula onto four warmed plates. Spoon some
of the juices over the top and serve with steamed
white rice and stir-fried Chinese greens. Serves 4

sweet and sour prawns

banana leaf fish

148

coconut snapper

spiced salmon

4 tablespoons olive oil
1 tablespoon ground cumin
1 teaspoon smoked paprika
1 teaspoon chilli flakes
juice of 2 limes
1 tablespoon small salted capers, rinsed and drained
1 tablespoon finely chopped preserved lemon rind
2 tablespoons finely chopped coriander (cilantro)
4 x 150 g (5^1/2 oz) salmon steaks
steamed couscous (Basics), to serve
small mint leaves, to serve

Put the olive oil, cumin, paprika, chilli flakes, lime juice, capers, preserved lemon rind and coriander in a bowl and stir to combine. Line a baking tray with foil and lay the salmon steaks over the top. Spoon the spice mixture over the salmon, then cover with plastic wrap and refrigerate for 1 hour.

Preheat the oven to 180°C (350°F/Gas 4). Bake the salmon for 10 minutes, or until cooked to your liking. Serve with steamed couscous and a scattering of mint. Serves 4

lobster salad

1 teaspoon ground coriander
1 teaspoon ground cumin
1 large red chilli, seeded and finely chopped
^{1}/2 teaspoon paprika
1 handful coriander (cilantro) leaves
1 handful flat-leaf (Italian) parsley
6 mint leaves
1 garlic clove
1 tablespoon balsamic vinegar
125 ml (4 fl oz/^{1}/2 cup) olive oil
2 cooked lobster tails
3 ripe tomatoes
2 roasted red capsicums (peppers), seeds, membranes and skin removed (Basics)
100 g (3^1/2 oz/2^3/4 cups) rocket (arugula) leaves

Put the ground coriander and cumin in a blender or food processor with the chilli, paprika, coriander leaves, parsley, mint, garlic, vinegar and 3 tablespoons of the olive oil. Blend to a smooth paste. With the motor running, slowly add the remaining oil to make a dressing.

Remove the shell from the lobster tails, finely slice the meat and toss it in a bowl with the dressing. Roughly chop the tomatoes, slice the capsicum into thin strips and toss them through the lobster. Arrange the rocket on four plates and pile the lobster salad over the top. Serves 4

make a splash with spicy salmon and refreshing mint

Opposite: spiced salmon
Over: lobster salad

mauritian fish stew

mauritian fish stew

2 dried limes
1 tablespoon olive oil
1 tablespoon ground cumin
1 tablespoon ground turmeric
1 garlic clove, crushed
1 large red chilli, seeded and finely chopped
1/2 vanilla bean
2 large ripe tomatoes, cut into 1 cm (1/2 inch)
    cubes
1 green capsicum (pepper), cut into 1 cm
    (1/2 inch) cubes
800 g (1 lb 12 oz) sea perch, kingfish or cod,
    cut into 3 cm (1 1/4 inch) wide strips
1 handful coriander (cilantro) sprigs
lime wedges, to serve

Pierce the dried limes several times with a needle. Heat the olive oil in a large heavy-based frying pan over medium heat and add the cumin, turmeric and garlic. Stir until the spices begin to brown, then add the dried limes, chilli, vanilla bean, tomato, capsicum and 500 ml (17 fl oz/2 cups) of water. Simmer over low heat for 20 minutes to allow the flavours to develop. Season to taste with sea salt.

Add the fish strips, then cover and cook for a further 10 minutes, or until the fish is cooked through. Divide the fish among four bowls and spoon the broth over the top. Scatter with coriander sprigs and serve with lime wedges. Serves 4

red snapper with tomato salsa

250 g (9 oz) cherry tomatoes, cut into quarters
1 teaspoon finely grated fresh ginger
2 tablespoons finely diced red onion
6 basil leaves, finely sliced
1 1/2 tablespoons lime juice
1 1/2 tablespoons coconut cream
2 tablespoons vegetable oil
4 x 200 g (7 oz) red snapper fillets, skin on
lime wedges, to serve

Preheat the oven to 200°C (400°F/Gas 6). To make the tomato salsa, put the cherry tomatoes, ginger, onion, basil, lime juice and coconut cream in a small bowl. Mix together and set aside.

Put the oil in a large heavy-based frying pan over high heat. Rinse the snapper fillets in cold water and pat dry with paper towels. Season liberally with sea salt and put the fillets, skin side down, in the hot pan. Sear for 1–2 minutes, or until the skin is crisp and golden, then turn the fillets over.

Lift the fish, skin side up, onto a baking tray lined with foil. Bake for 8–10 minutes, or until cooked through. Lift the fillets into a serving dish, then spoon the salsa over the top and serve with lime wedges. Serves 4

a bowl brimming with enticing island spices

red snapper with tomato salsa

157

chunky tomato, olive and basil salsa

For a fresh and easy Mediterranean-style salsa, slice
12 cherry tomatoes in half (or into quarters if large) and
put them in a bowl with 10 torn basil leaves, 12 small
black olives, 1 1/2 tablespoons balsamic vinegar and
3 tablespoons extra virgin olive oil. Season with sea
salt and freshly ground black pepper. Toss together
and spoon over grilled (broiled) tuna, swordfish or
marlin, drizzling any remaining dressing over the top.
Makes about 200 g (7 oz/1 1/2 cups)

green sauce

For a green sauce that's perfect with white fish, pile
1 large handful of coriander (cilantro) leaves onto a
chopping board with 10 mint leaves, 1 tablespoon
rinsed and drained small salted capers, 1 crushed
garlic clove and 1 seeded and roughly chopped long
green chilli. Using a sharp knife, chop all the ingredients
together to form a rough paste. Put the paste in a
bowl and add 1 tablespoon lime juice, 1 teaspoon fish
sauce and 4 tablespoons olive oil. Mix together and
spoon over baked or steamed blue-eye cod, snapper
or john dory. Makes about 75 g (2 1/2 oz/1/2 cup)

lime and avocado salsa

For a quick, zingy salsa, put 1 diced ripe avocado in a bowl with 1 finely chopped Lebanese (short) cucumber, 1/2 small finely diced red onion, 2 seeded and finely chopped large red chillies, 1 large handful coriander (cilantro) leaves, 2 teaspoons fish sauce, 2 tablespoons lime juice and 4 tablespoons olive oil. Using a sharp knife, cut the top and base off 1 lime. Sit the lime on a chopping board and run the knife down all sides, removing the skin and pith. Run the knife between the membranes to release the lime segments, then finely chop them and gently stir them into the salsa, being careful not to mash the avocado. Serve with grilled (broiled) fish. Makes about 600 g (1 lb 5 oz/2 cups)

lime pickle sauce

For a piquant sauce with a taste of India, put a generous handful of parsley in a food processor with 4 anchovies, 1 teaspoon drained and rinsed small salted capers, 10 mint leaves, 2 tablespoons Indian lime pickle and 4 tablespoons light olive oil. Blend into a sauce. Serve with grilled (broiled) white fish, such as blue-eye cod, and boiled potatoes. Makes about 75 g (2 1/2 oz/1/2 cup)

husk

golden grains   slippery noodles

bowls of bounty   savoury and sweet

A drizzle of sauce, a sprinkle of spice and a golden burst of citrus tang is all it takes to bring simple grains to life. Their purpose is to soak up flavour, add texture and crunch or bring a comforting richness to a humble meal. They may revel in simple, salty sauces, but these simple staples also come into their own at dessert time with a spoonful of sugar and a dollop of cream. So break bread, slurp a noodle, twirl your pasta, scoop the rice, spice the couscous and enjoy the sizzle of batter as it hits the pan.

pineapple and lime muffins

215 g (7^1/$_2$ oz/1^3/$_4$ cups) plain (all-purpose) flour
2 heaped teaspoons baking powder
165 g (5^3/$_4$ oz/^{3}/$_4$ cup) sugar
^{1}/$_4$ teaspoon ground cardamom
pinch of ground cloves
115 g (4 oz/1^1/$_4$ cups) desiccated coconut
2 tablespoons unsalted butter, melted
125 ml (4 fl oz/^{1}/$_2$ cup) coconut milk
grated zest and juice of 2 limes
2 eggs
190 g (6^3/$_4$ oz/1 cup) diced fresh pineapple

Preheat the oven to 180°C (350°F/Gas 4). Sift the flour, baking powder and a pinch of salt into a mixing bowl. Stir in the sugar, cardamom, cloves and coconut.

Make a well in the centre and add the melted butter, coconut milk, lime zest, lime juice and eggs. Mix until just combined, then fold the pineapple through.

Spoon into 10 holes of a greased standard muffin tin and bake for 25 minutes, or until a skewer inserted in the middle comes out clean. Makes 10

berry breakfast trifle

200 g (7 oz/2 cups) rolled (porridge) oats
250 ml (9 fl oz/1 cup) apple juice
500 g (1 lb 2 oz/3^1/$_3$ cups) strawberries, hulled
3 teaspoons honey
125 g (4^1/$_2$ oz/^{1}/$_2$ cup) plain yoghurt
150 g (5^1/$_2$ oz/1 cup) blueberries

Put the oats and apple juice in a bowl, mix well, then cover with plastic wrap. Cover and refrigerate for at least 1 hour or overnight, to allow the oats to soak.

Mash half the strawberries with the honey, then mix them through the soaked oats along with the yoghurt. Slice the remaining strawberries.

Spoon half the oat mixture into four serving glasses, and top with half the berries. Cover with the remaining oat mixture, then top with the remaining berries. Serves 4

rise and shine with the sweet bite of pineapple and lime

Opposite: pineapple and lime muffins

berry breakfast trifle

fried egg and aromatic rice

2 tablespoons butter
2 garlic cloves, crushed
1 red onion, finely diced
1 tablespoon finely chopped lemon grass,
    white part only
1 tablespoon finely chopped fresh ginger
370 g (13 oz/2 cups) cooked basmati rice
2 tablespoons olive oil
4 eggs
2 handfuls coriander (cilantro) leaves,
    roughly chopped
1 handful parsley, roughly chopped
25 g (1 oz/1 bunch) chives, finely snipped
sweet chilli sauce (Basics), to serve

Melt the butter in a large heavy-based saucepan
or wok over medium heat. Add the garlic, onion,
lemon grass and ginger and cook, stirring often, for
5 minutes, or until the onion is soft and lightly golden.
Add the rice and cook, stirring, for 5 minutes, or until
all the ingredients are well combined and the rice is
starting to stick to the base of the pan. Remove from
the heat and set aside.

Heat the olive oil in a large frying pan over medium–high
heat and fry the eggs to your liking. Stir the coriander,
parsley and chives through the rice and divide among
four shallow bowls. Top each bowl with a fried egg
and serve with sweet chilli sauce. Serves 4

breakfast bars

150 g (5^1/$_2$ oz) butter
175 g (6 oz/^{1}/$_2$ cup) honey
200 g (7 oz/2 cups) rolled (porridge) oats
60 g (2^1/$_4$ oz/1 cup) shredded coconut
1 teaspoon baking powder
3 tablespoons sesame seeds
200 g (7 oz/^{3}/$_4$ cup) pitted prunes, chopped
100 g (3^1/$_2$ oz/^{2}/$_3$ cup) dried peaches, chopped
75 g (2^1/$_2$ oz/^{1}/$_2$ cup) currants
3 eggs

Preheat the oven to 170°C (325°F/Gas 3). Line
a 23 × 32 cm (9 × 12^3/$_4$ inch) sandwich tin with
baking paper.

Put the butter and honey in a small saucepan over
medium heat and stir until the butter has melted.

Toss the oats, coconut, baking powder and sesame
seeds together in a large bowl. Add the prunes,
peaches and currants and mix well. Add the warm
honey mixture and eggs and stir to combine, then
spoon evenly into the sandwich tin.

Bake for 25–30 minutes, or until the mixture is cooked
through and the top is golden brown. Remove from
the oven and allow to cool in the tin before cutting
into 12 bars. Makes 12

mid-morning soul food with a dash of chilli

fried egg and aromatic rice

breakfast bars

sliced leg ham with a burghul salad

sliced leg ham with a burghul salad

10 bulb spring onions (scallions)
1 tablespoon balsamic vinegar
1 tablespoon olive oil
1 tablespoon caster (superfine) sugar
500 g (1 lb 2 oz) cherry tomatoes
90 g (3¼ oz/½ cup) burghul (bulgur)
1 teaspoon ground cumin
zest and juice of 1 lemon
2 tablespoons extra virgin olive oil
2 handfuls flat-leaf (Italian) parsley, roughly chopped
8–12 slices leg ham, off the bone

Preheat the oven to 180°C (350°F/Gas 4). Trim the onions and slice them in half lengthways. Toss them in a bowl with the vinegar, olive oil and sugar until all the onions are thoroughly coated. Spread them on a baking tray lined with foil and bake for 25 minutes, or until golden brown.

Add the cherry tomatoes to the baking tray and roast for another 5–10 minutes, or until the skins are starting to split. Remove from the oven.

Put the burghul and cumin in a bowl and cover with 125 ml (4 fl oz/½ cup) of boiling water. Leave to sit for 10 minutes, to allow the grains to soak up the water.

Add the roasted onions and tomatoes, lemon zest, lemon juice, extra virgin olive oil and parsley. Season to taste with sea salt and freshly ground black pepper and toss to combine. Divide the ham among four plates and spoon the salad over the top. Serves 4

citrus couscous

185 g (6½ oz/1 cup) instant couscous
1 teaspoon grated orange zest
juice of 1 orange
1 teaspoon grated lemon zest
juice of 1 lemon
2 tablespoons olive oil
2 tablespoons finely chopped preserved lemon rind
2 Lebanese (short) cucumbers, peeled and finely diced
20 basil leaves

Put the couscous in a large bowl and pour 250 ml (9 fl oz/1 cup) of boiling water over the top. Cover and allow to sit for 5 minutes, then fluff up the grains with a fork. Cover again and leave for a further 5 minutes. When the couscous has absorbed all the water, rub the grains with your fingertips to remove any lumps.

In a small bowl, combine the orange zest, orange juice, lemon zest, lemon juice, olive oil and preserved lemon rind. Pour the mixture over the couscous, add the cucumber and basil and toss to combine. Season with sea salt and freshly ground black pepper. Serve with smoked or roast chicken or chargrilled fish.
Serves 4

boiled egg and quinoa salad

1 egg yolk
1 tablespoon lemon juice
125 ml (4 fl oz/½ cup) light olive oil
2 anchovy fillets, finely chopped
4 eggs, at room temperature
100 g (3½ oz/½ cup) quinoa
75 g (2½ oz/2¼ cups) wild rocket (arugula) leaves
1 tablespoon finely snipped chives

In a small bowl, whisk together the egg yolk and lemon juice, then slowly whisk in the olive oil to make a dressing. Whisk in the anchovies, then season to taste with sea salt and freshly ground black pepper.

Bring a saucepan of water to the boil and add the eggs. Boil the eggs for 5 minutes, then lift them out of the water and leave to cool.

Put the quinoa in a saucepan and cover with 500 ml (17 fl oz/2 cups) of water. Bring to the boil, then reduce the heat and simmer for 5 minutes, or until the grains are cooked through. Drain the quinoa, tip it into a bowl and stir through half the anchovy dressing.

Arrange a nest of rocket leaves on four plates, then spoon a pile of quinoa into the middle. Peel the eggs, slice them in half and sit them on the quinoa. Drizzle with the remaining dressing and sprinkle with the chives. Serves 4

sand between the toes, an idyllic view and a golden lunch

citrus couscous

boiled egg and quinoa salad

crunchy noodle salad

crunchy noodle salad

1 tablespoon grated palm sugar or soft brown sugar
2 teaspoons balsamic vinegar
1 tablespoon kecap manis
1 large red chilli, seeded and finely chopped
2 garlic cloves, finely chopped
80 g (2³/4 oz/¹/2 cup) peanuts, toasted and ground
125 ml (4 fl oz/¹/2 cup) peanut oil
90 g (3¹/4 oz) dried Chinese egg vermicelli
2 witlof (chicory/Belgian endive), leaves separated
2 Lebanese (short) cucumbers, cut into long,
    thin strips
2 carrots, peeled and cut into long, thin strips
12 cherry tomatoes, cut in half
100 g (3¹/2 oz) deep-fried tofu, thinly sliced
4 boiled eggs, peeled and cut in half

Put the sugar in a bowl with 3 tablespoons of boiling water. Stir until the sugar has dissolved, then add the vinegar, kecap manis, chilli, garlic and ground peanuts. Stir well to make a peanut sauce.

Heat the peanut oil in a wok or small saucepan over high heat. When it begins to shimmer, add some of the vermicelli by crumbling the nest into broken strands. Fry for a minute or two, or until the threads begin to look golden brown rather than yellow. Remove with a slotted spoon and drain on paper towels — you'll probably need to fry the vermicelli in several batches.

Divide the witlof leaves among four plates and top with the vermicelli. Add the cucumber, carrot, cherry tomatoes and tofu. Top with the boiled egg halves and drizzle with the peanut sauce. Serves 4

capsicum curry

2 tablespoons olive oil
2 garlic cloves, crushed
1 tablespoon grated fresh ginger
1 tablespoon black mustard seeds
¹/2 teaspoon cumin seeds
¹/4 teaspoon ground cloves
¹/2 teaspoon ground turmeric
2 red onions, finely sliced
2 large red chillies, seeded and finely chopped
2 tablespoons tomato paste (concentrated purée)
250 ml (9 fl oz/1 cup) coconut milk
1 red capsicum (pepper), finely sliced
1 green capsicum (pepper), finely sliced
1 yellow capsicum (pepper), finely sliced
2 handfuls coriander (cilantro) leaves
chapatti, steamed white rice (Basics) or nutty rice
    (page 184), to serve

Heat the olive oil in a large saucepan over medium–high heat. Add the garlic, ginger, mustard seeds, cumin seeds, cloves and turmeric. Cook for 1 minute, or until the mustard seeds begin to pop, then add the onion and chilli. Cook, stirring, for 3 minutes, or until the onion has softened.

Stir in the tomato paste, coconut milk and all the capsicum and reduce the heat to low. Cook for a further 20 minutes, or until the capsicums are soft. Season with sea salt if needed, then take the pan off the heat and stir through the coriander leaves. Serve with rice or chapatti. Serves 4

salad with the lot: bite, crunch, sweet, sour, cool and hot

capsicum curry

fresh tomato pasta

4 medium–large, very ripe tomatoes
1 teaspoon sea salt
2 tablespoons small salted capers, rinsed and drained
15 basil leaves, finely chopped
1 handful flat-leaf (Italian) parsley, roughly chopped
500 g (1 lb 2 oz) casareccia or penne
75 g (2 1/2 oz/3/4 cup) finely grated parmesan cheese
3 tablespoons olive oil
20 niçoise olives
finely grated parmesan cheese, extra, to serve

Chop the tomatoes and put them in a bowl with the sea salt, capers, basil and parsley. Stir gently to coat the tomatoes, then set aside.

Bring a large pot of salted water to the boil and cook the pasta until *al dente*. Drain the pasta, then return to the warm pot. Add the parmesan and olive oil and stir a few times, before adding the tomatoes. Season with freshly ground black pepper, toss together, then divide among four pasta bowls. Scatter with the olives and sprinkle with some extra parmesan. Serves 4

nutty rice

2 tablespoons olive oil
1 teaspoon cumin seeds
1 tablespoon sesame seeds
200 g (7 oz/1 cup) basmati rice
1 handful coriander (cilantro) leaves,
    roughly chopped

Heat the olive oil in a large saucepan over medium heat. Add the cumin and sesame seeds and fry for 1 minute, or until the sesame seeds turn golden brown.

Add the rice and cook for 1 minute, then pour in 500 ml (17 fl oz/2 cups) of water and bring to the boil, stirring occasionally.

Cover the pan and reduce the heat to low. Simmer for 15 minutes, or until the rice is fluffy and cooked through. Quickly stir in the coriander and serve with a capsicum curry (page 181), or chargrilled prawns (shrimp) or fish. Serves 4

ripe ruby-red tomatoes singing of the sun

Opposite: fresh tomato pasta

nutty rice

crab and lemon pasta

350 g (12 oz/2½ cups) fresh crabmeat
2 large red chillies, seeded and finely chopped
grated zest and juice of 1 lemon
4 tablespoons extra virgin olive oil
1 handful flat-leaf (Italian) parsley, roughly chopped
300 g (10½ oz/2 bunches) rocket (arugula), stalks
    removed, leaves finely sliced
400 g (14 oz) spaghettini

Put the crabmeat in a large bowl and roughly flake it with a fork. Add the chilli, lemon zest, lemon juice and olive oil. Season liberally with sea salt and freshly ground black pepper and stir to combine. Pile the parsley and rocket over the top.

Bring a large pot of salted water to the boil and add the spaghettini. Cook until *al dente*, then drain and add to the crab mixture. Toss well until the rocket has wilted, then divide among four warmed pasta bowls. Serves 4

simmered vegetables and tofu

1 garlic clove, finely sliced
2 tablespoons soy sauce
2 teaspoons sesame oil
125 ml (4 fl oz/½ cup) shaoxing rice wine
125 ml (4 fl oz/½ cup) mirin
2 star anise
1 tablespoon finely sliced fresh ginger
12 fresh shiitake mushrooms, cut in half if large
1 red capsicum (pepper), cut into 1 cm (½ inch) cubes
1 yellow capsicum (pepper), cut into 1 cm
    (½ inch) cubes
300 g (10½ oz) silken tofu
2 spring onions (scallions), finely sliced on
    the diagonal
steamed white rice (Basics), nutty rice (page 184)
    or brown rice, to serve

Put the garlic, soy sauce, sesame oil, rice wine, mirin, star anise, ginger, mushrooms and all the capsicum in a large saucepan. Add 125 ml (4 fl oz/½ cup) of water and bring to the boil over high heat. Reduce the heat to low and allow the broth to simmer for 10 minutes.

Cut the tofu into 1.5 cm (⅝ inch) cubes and divide among four wide, warmed bowls. Spoon the vegetables and broth over the top. Garnish with spring onion and serve with rice. Serves 4

tuna and quinoa salad

150 g (5½ oz/¾ cup) quinoa
2 tablespoons lemon juice
2 tablespoons olive oil
1 tablespoon finely chopped preserved lemon rind
25 g (1 oz/1 bunch) chives, finely snipped
200 g (7 oz) green beans, blanched and cut into
    3 cm (1¼ inch) lengths, on the diagonal
250 g (9 oz) cherry tomatoes, cut into quarters
200 g (7 oz) tinned tuna in oil, drained
40 g (1½ oz/1¼ cups) mizuna or baby salad leaves

Put the quinoa in a saucepan and cover with 500 ml (17 fl oz/2 cups) of water. Bring to the boil, then reduce the heat and simmer for 5 minutes, or until the grains are cooked through. Remove from the heat and drain.

Put the lemon juice, olive oil, preserved lemon rind and chives in a bowl and add the quinoa. Toss together, then add the green beans, cherry tomatoes and tuna. Toss once more and season to taste with sea salt and freshly ground black pepper. Divide the salad leaves among four plates and spoon the tuna and quinoa salad over the top. Serves 4

a simple pasta worthy of a crystal sea and a clear blue sky

Opposite: crab and lemon pasta

simmered vegetables and tofu

tuna and quinoa salad

buckwheat noodle salad

Put 3 teaspoons dashi granules in a large bowl with
4 tablespoons soy sauce, 4 tablespoons mirin and
1 teaspoon sugar. Stir to make a dressing. Bring a
large pot of water to the boil and add 300 g (10½ oz)
buckwheat noodles. Cook until *al dente*, then drain,
rinse and toss them through the dressing to coat. Add
2 finely sliced spring onions (scallions), 1 diced red
capsicum (pepper) and 150 g (5½ oz) trimmed snow
peas (mangetout), finely sliced on the diagonal. Toss
well, then divide among four bowls. Using tongs, pass
a nori sheet over a gas flame several times to roast it,
or crisp it in a hot oven for a few minutes, then cut
it into fine 4 cm (1½ inch) long strips with kitchen
scissors. Drizzle the salads with any remaining
dressing and garnish with the nori strips. Serves 4

shiitake broth with somen noodles

Soak 8 dried shiitake mushrooms in 500 ml (17 fl oz/
2 cups) hot water for 30 minutes. Drain the liquid into
a saucepan, finely slice the mushrooms and add them
to the pan with 2 teaspoons dashi granules, 1 litre
(35 fl oz/4 cups) water, 3 tablespoons white miso
paste and 3 tablespoons soy sauce. Bring to the boil,
then reduce the heat and simmer for 10 minutes. Add
12 chopped baby corn cobs and cook for 3 minutes,
then add 175 g (6 oz/1 bunch) chopped asparagus
and cook for 3 minutes. Meanwhile, cook 200 g (7 oz)
somen noodles in a large pot of boiling water for
3 minutes, then drain, rinse and divide among four
warmed bowls. Spoon the shiitake broth over the
top and scatter with 2 finely sliced spring onions
(scallions). Serves 4

buckwheat noodle and herb salad

Put 1¹/₂ tablespoons soy sauce in a large bowl with
1¹/₂ tablespoons sesame oil, 2 teaspoons balsamic
vinegar, 1 tablespoon caster (superfine) sugar,
2 tablespoons lime juice and 1 tablespoon finely
chopped lemon grass (white part only). Stir to make
a dressing. Bring a large pot of water to the boil and
add 300 g (10¹/₂ oz) buckwheat noodles. Cook until
al dente, then drain, rinse and toss them through the
dressing to coat. Add half a peeled and finely julienned
daikon, 2 heaped tablespoons finely julienned fresh
ginger, 1 handful mint and 2 handfuls coriander
(cilantro) leaves. Gently toss together, then pile the
noodles into four bowls. Serves 4

fresh egg noodle salad

Bring a large pot of salted water to the boil and add
200 g (7 oz) fresh egg noodles. Cook until *al dente*,
then drain, rinse and set aside. In a large bowl, toss
together 45 g (1¹/₂ oz/1 cup) finely sliced Chinese
cabbage, 2 finely sliced spring onions (scallions), 100 g
(3¹/₂ oz/1 heaped cup) bean sprouts, 1 julienned carrot,
1 julienned red capsicum (pepper) and 2 handfuls
coriander (cilantro) leaves. In a small bowl, combine
3 tablespoons hoisin sauce, 1¹/₂ tablespoons lime
juice, 1 teaspoon sesame oil and 1 teaspoon sugar,
then pour over the vegetables. Rinse and drain the
noodles, then toss them through the salad and divide
among four bowls. Serve sprinkled with 2 tablespoons
toasted sesame seeds. Serves 4

caramelized chicken breast

3 tablespoons vegetable oil
4 boneless chicken breasts, skin on
3 French or red Asian shallots, finely chopped
3 tablespoons caster (superfine) sugar
3 tablespoons fish sauce
1 tablespoon finely grated fresh ginger
1/4 teaspoon ground white pepper
2 small Lebanese (short) cucumbers, finely sliced
2 witlof (chicory/Belgian endive), leaves separated
25 g (1 oz/1 bunch) chives, finely snipped
20 mint leaves
1 tablespoon lime juice
steamed coconut rice (Basics) or steamed white
    rice (Basics), to serve

Heat the oil in a large heavy-based frying pan over medium–high heat. Add the chicken breasts, skin side down, and cook for 3 minutes, or until golden brown. Turn and cook the other side for 2 minutes, then remove the chicken from the pan.

Add the shallots to the pan and cook for 1 minute over medium heat. Add the sugar and cook for a further 2 minutes, or until the shallots are golden brown. Stir in the fish sauce, ginger and white pepper and cook for 1 minute.

Put the chicken back in, skin side up. Cover the pan, reduce the heat to low and cook for 12–15 minutes, or until the chicken is cooked through. Take the pan off the heat and keep the chicken warm while preparing the salad.

In a bowl, toss together the cucumber, witlof, chives, mint and lime juice. Season with sea salt.

Serve the salad in four large bowls, piled over some steamed coconut rice or steamed white rice, with thick slices of chicken breast arranged over the top. Spoon the caramelized shallots and pan juices over the chicken just before serving. Serves 4

seared beef and noodle salad

zest and juice of 2 limes
zest and juice of 1 orange
2 tablespoons fish sauce
1 teaspoon sesame oil
1 tablespoon grated palm sugar or soft brown sugar
1 garlic clove, crushed
2 tablespoons finely chopped lemon grass,
    white part only
1 tablespoon julienned fresh ginger
1 large red chilli, seeded and finely sliced
2 tablespoons olive oil
250 g (9 oz) piece of beef sirloin
200 g (7 oz) somen noodles
1 handful coriander (cilantro) leaves
1 handful Thai basil

In a small bowl, mix together the lime zest, lime juice, orange zest, orange juice, fish sauce, sesame oil, sugar, garlic, lemon grass, ginger and chilli. Stir until the sugar has dissolved, then cover the dressing and set aside until ready to use.

Heat the olive oil in a frying pan over high heat and add the beef. Cook on each side for 2–3 minutes, or until well seared. Transfer the meat to a bowl, cover loosely with foil and leave to rest.

Bring a large pot of salted water to the boil. Add the noodles and cook for 2 minutes, then drain and rinse under running water. Put the noodles in a large bowl and pour half the dressing over. Toss well to coat, then divide the noodles among four bowls.

Finely slice the beef and arrange over the noodles. Scatter with the coriander and basil and spoon the remaining dressing over the top. Serves 4

a bowl of succulent chicken, sticky with asian flavours

Opposite: caramelized chicken breast
Over: seared beef and noodle salad

195

rice noodle rolls with ginger chicken

rice noodle rolls with ginger chicken

500 g (1 lb 2 oz) fresh rice noodle sheets,
   at room temperature
1 tablespoon peanut oil
1 teaspoon finely chopped lemon grass,
   white part only
1 teaspoon finely grated fresh ginger
1 boneless, skinless chicken breast, finely diced
250 g (9 oz) baby English spinach leaves
2 tablespoons finely snipped garlic chives
2 tablespoons vegetable oil
sweet chilli sauce (Basics), to serve

Open out the rice noodle sheets and cut out eight
20 cm (8 inch) squares. Put them in a bowl, cover
with hot water and leave to soften.

Heat the peanut oil in a wok and add the lemon grass,
ginger and chicken. Stir-fry over medium heat for
5 minutes, or until the chicken is cooked. Add the
baby spinach, toss until the leaves are just wilted,
then take the wok off the heat. Allow the mixture to
cool, then stir through the garlic chives.

Drain the noodle sheets and pat dry with paper
towels. Spoon the chicken mixture along the centre
of each noodle sheet and roll them up by folding the
edges over each other.

Heat the vegetable oil in a non-stick frying pan. Working
in two batches, cook the noodle rolls for 1 minute on
each side, or until lightly golden. Serve warm with
sweet chilli sauce. Serves 4

ginger panna cotta

400 ml (14 fl oz) cream (whipping)
grated zest and juice of 1 lemon
1 tablespoon finely grated fresh ginger
50 g (1¾ oz/scant ¼ cup) caster (superfine) sugar
1½ gelatine leaves
1 tablespoon Grand Marnier or orange-flavoured
   liqueur
cardamom almond bread (Basics) or pistachio
   biscotti (Basics), to serve

Whip 150 ml (5 fl oz) of the cream in a bowl, cover
with plastic wrap and refrigerate until needed.

Put the remaining cream in a saucepan with the lemon
zest, lemon juice and ginger and heat gently over low
heat for 10 minutes, or until slightly thickened — do not
let the cream come to the boil. Strain into a bowl.

Soak the gelatine leaves in a bowl of cold water for
5 minutes, or until dissolved to a jellied consistency.
Squeeze the excess water from the gelatine leaves
and stir them into the warm cream mixture along with
the Grand Marnier. Leave for about 40 minutes to
cool, then fold through the whipped cream.

Spoon the panna cotta into four small bowls, then cover
and refrigerate for 3 hours or overnight. Serve with
cardamom almond bread or pistachio biscotti. Serves 4

fragrant peach tart

6–7 small ripe peaches
25 cm (10 inch) prebaked shortcrust tart case,
   with 3 cm (1¼ inch) deep sides (Basics)
2 eggs
115 g (4 oz/½ cup) caster (superfine) sugar
4 tablespoons plain (all-purpose) flour
½ teaspoon rosewater
110 g (3¾ oz) unsalted butter
thick (double/heavy) cream, to serve

Preheat the oven to 180°C (350°F/Gas 4). Slice the
peaches in half and remove the stones. Slice the flesh
into thick wedges and arrange in the base of the tart
case, cut sides up.

Crack the eggs into a mixing bowl, add the sugar and
beat with electric beaters until pale and fluffy. Fold in
the flour and rosewater.

Heat the butter in a saucepan over high heat. When
it begins to froth and turn pale golden brown, pour it
into the egg mixture and beat for 1 minute. Pour the
filling over the peaches and bake for 35 minutes. Cover
the tart with foil and bake for a further 15 minutes, or
until the filling has set. Allow the tart to cool and serve
with cream. Serves 8

coconut and passionfruit bavarois

250 ml (9 fl oz/1 cup) cream (whipping)
300 ml (10½ fl oz) milk
45 g (1½ oz/½ cup) desiccated coconut
125 g (4½ oz/heaped ½ cup) caster (superfine) sugar
4 egg yolks
2 gelatine leaves
4 passionfruit
cardamom almond bread (Basics) or pistachio
   biscotti (Basics), to serve

Whip the cream in a bowl, cover with plastic wrap
and refrigerate until needed.

Put the milk in a heavy-based saucepan over very low
heat and stir in the coconut and sugar. Allow the milk
to just simmer for 15 minutes, or until reduced and
thick, then strain into a bowl through a fine sieve.
Using the back of a large spoon, press as much liquid
as possible out of the coconut, into the bowl.

Whisk the egg yolks in a separate bowl, then whisk in
the warm milk. Pour into a clean saucepan and stir over
medium heat for 8–10 minutes, or until the mixture
coats the back of the spoon. Pour into a clean bowl.

Soak the gelatine leaves in a bowl of cold water for
5 minutes, or until dissolved to a jellied consistency.
Squeeze the excess water from the gelatine leaves
and add them to the hot milk mixture. Whisk for a
few minutes to ensure the gelatine has completely
dissolved. Leave for 45 minutes, or until cool.

Fold the whipped cream through the mixture and spoon
into four serving glasses. Cover with plastic wrap and
chill for 3 hours, or overnight. Just before serving, slice
the passionfruit in half, scoop out the seeds and spoon
them over the top. Serve with cardamom almond
bread or pistachio biscotti. Serves 4

Opposite: ginger panna cotta
Over: fragrant peach tart; coconut and passionfruit bavarois

chocolate plum cake

chocolate plum cake

165 g (5³/4 oz/³/4 cup firmly packed) dark brown sugar
280 g (10 oz/2¹/4 cups) plain (all-purpose) flour
185 g (6¹/2 oz) unsalted butter
2 teaspoons baking powder
3 tablespoons dark cocoa powder
¹/4 teaspoon salt
230 g (8 oz/1 cup) caster (superfine) sugar
3 eggs, lightly beaten
185 ml (6 fl oz/³/4 cup) milk
16 small plums (550 g/1 lb 4 oz in total),
    stones removed, cut in half
ice cream or thick (double/heavy) cream, to serve

Preheat the oven to 180°C (350°F/Gas 4). Put the brown sugar in a bowl with 30 g (1 oz/¹/4 cup) of the flour and mix together. Add 3 tablespoons of the cold butter (leave the rest at room temperature to soften) and rub the butter in with your fingertips until the mixture resembles coarse breadcrumbs.

Sift the remaining flour into a mixing bowl along with the baking powder, cocoa powder and salt. Put the caster sugar and softened butter in a separate bowl and cream together using electric beaters, then add the eggs and mix well. Add half the flour mixture, then half the milk, mixing well after each addition. Mix in the remaining flour mixture, then the remaining milk.

Pour the cake batter into a greased 25 cm (10 inch) spring-form cake tin and arrange the plum halves on top, cut sides down. Sprinkle with the brown sugar mixture and bake for 50–60 minutes, or until a skewer inserted in the middle comes out clean.

Remove the cake from the oven and allow to cool before turning out of the tin. Serve with ice cream or cream. Serves 10

honey and almond cakes

100 g (3¹/2 oz/heaped ³/4 cup) slivered almonds
200 g (7 oz/scant ²/3 cup) clear honey
3 large eggs, separated
100 g (3¹/2 oz/heaped ³/4 cup) plain (all-purpose) flour
1 teaspoon baking powder
100 ml (3¹/2 fl oz) cream (whipping)
1¹/2 teaspoons orange flower water
icing (confectioners') sugar, for dusting
thick (double/heavy) cream, to serve
fresh raspberries and blackberries, to serve

Preheat the oven to 180°C (350°F/Gas 4). Grease an 18 cm (7 inch) square cake tin and line it with baking paper.

Put the almonds in a food processor and pulse a few times to grind them into a coarse powder.

Pour the honey into a small saucepan and gently heat over low heat. Whisk the egg yolks in a bowl until pale and creamy, then add the warm honey and mix well. Add the flour, baking powder and ground almonds, then stir in the cream and orange flower water.

Whisk the egg whites until soft peaks form, then lightly fold them into the cake mixture. Pour into the cake tin and bake for 30–35 minutes, or until lightly golden.

Remove the cake from the oven and allow to cool in the tin. Turn the cake out, dust with icing sugar and cut into nine squares. Serve topped with a dollop of cream and a tumble of fresh berries. Serves 9

late summer plums baked into chocolatey perfection

Over: honey and almond cakes

cinnamon pikelets

Mix 1½ tablespoons lime juice with 100 ml (3½ fl oz) maple syrup and set aside. In a large bowl, mix together 125 g (4½ oz/1 cup) plain (all-purpose) flour, 1 teaspoon ground cinnamon, 1 heaped teaspoon baking powder and 2 tablespoons caster (superfine) sugar and make a well in the centre. Stir in 1 egg whisked with 185 ml (6 fl oz/¾ cup) milk, to make a smooth batter — if it is too thick, stir in an extra 2 tablespoons milk. Put a non-stick frying pan over medium heat and melt just enough butter to coat. Spoon in enough batter to form three 7–8 cm (3 inch) pikelets (griddle cakes). Cook for 20–30 seconds, or until the top begins to bubble, then flip and cook for 30 seconds, then remove. Repeat with the remaining batter, adding more butter to the pan each time. Serve layered with banana slices and drizzled with the maple and lime syrup. Serves 4

chocolate and hazelnut cookies

Melt 150 g (5½ oz) good-quality dark chocolate and 4 tablespoons unsalted butter in a small saucepan over low heat. Add 200 g (7 oz/1 heaped cup lightly packed) dark brown sugar and stir for 1 minute, or until the sugar dissolves. Sift in 100 g (3½ oz/heaped ¾ cup) plain (all-purpose) flour, then stir in 1 teaspoon natural vanilla extract and 55 g (2 oz/½ cup) ground hazelnuts. Add 1 egg, stir to form a thick dough, then cover with plastic wrap and refrigerate for 1 hour. Preheat the oven to 180°C (350°F/Gas 4). Shape the dough into small walnut-sized balls and bake on two baking trays lined with baking paper for 15–20 minutes, or until they look dry. Serve with cream and fresh figs marinated in brown sugar and Grand Marnier. Makes 30

coconut and lime pancakes

In a large bowl, mix together 125 g (4^1/$_2$ oz/1 cup) plain (all-purpose) flour, 1 heaped teaspoon baking powder and 2 tablespoons desiccated coconut. Make a well in the centre. In another bowl combine 3 tablespoons finely grated palm sugar or soft brown sugar, 1 egg, 3 tablespoons milk, 250 ml (9 fl oz/1 cup) coconut milk and the grated zest and juice of 1 lime. Whisk until the sugar has dissolved, then stir into the flour mixture to make a thick batter. Heat a large non-stick frying pan over medium heat and spoon in enough batter to form a 12 cm (4^1/$_2$ inch) pancake, smoothing the mixture over the base of the pan. Cook for 30 seconds, or until it looks dry, then flip and cook for 1 minute. Remove and make seven more pancakes. Serve wrapped around thin slices of fresh tropical fruits such as mango, pineapple and papaya. Makes 8

berry shortcakes

In a large bowl, mix together 185 g (6^1/$_2$ oz/1^1/$_2$ cups) plain (all-purpose) flour, ^{1}/$_2$ teaspoon salt, 2 teaspoons baking powder and 4 tablespoons caster (superfine) sugar. Add 100 g (3^1/$_2$ oz) butter, rubbing it in with your fingertips, then mix in 1 egg. Gather the mixture onto a sheet of plastic wrap, roll up into a fat log about 8 cm (3^1/$_4$ inches) in diameter and chill for 1 hour. Preheat the oven to 180°C (350°F/Gas 4). Cut the log into eight discs and put them on a baking tray lined with baking paper. Flatten them slightly, then bake for 10–12 minutes, or until golden brown. Remove from the oven and allow to cool on the tray. Dust with icing (confectioners') sugar and serve with whipped cream and a bowl of strawberries and raspberries. Serves 8

basics

couscous

185 g (6¹/₂ oz/1 cup) instant couscous
1 tablespoon butter

Put the couscous and butter in a large bowl and pour
250 ml (9 fl oz/1 cup) of boiling water over the top.
Cover and allow to sit for 5 minutes, then fluff up the
grains with a fork. Cover again and leave for a further
5 minutes. Season with a little sea salt and freshly
ground black pepper, then rub the grains with your
fingertips to remove any lumps. The couscous can
be served warm or chilled.

herbed couscous

185 g (6¹/₂ oz/1 cup) instant couscous
1 tablespoon butter
1 handful coriander (cilantro) leaves, roughly chopped
1 handful flat-leaf (Italian) parsley, roughly chopped
finely chopped basil (optional)
finely chopped mint (optional)
finely snipped chives (optional)

Put the couscous and butter in a large bowl and pour
250 ml (9 fl oz/1 cup) of boiling water over the top.
Cover and allow to sit for 5 minutes, then fluff up the
grains with a fork. Cover again and leave for a further
5 minutes. Season with a little sea salt and freshly
ground black pepper, then rub the grains with your
fingertips to remove any lumps.

Allow the couscous to cool a little, then stir through
the coriander and parsley. To vary the flavour, you can
also add some finely chopped basil, mint or chives,
to suit the dish you are serving the couscous with.
Serves 4 as a side dish

roasted capsicums

2–3 red capsicums (peppers)
olive oil, for brushing

Preheat the oven to 200°C (400°F/Gas 6). Sit a small
rack on or over a baking tray or roasting tin. Lightly rub
the capsicums with olive oil and sit them on the rack.

Roast the capsicums for 8–10 minutes, or until the
skins begin to blister and blacken — you may need
to turn them several times so the skins blister all over.
(If you have a gas stove you can also blister the skin
by carefully putting the capsicums directly over the
flame, turning them around as the skin blisters.) Put
the roasted capsicums in a container, cover with
plastic wrap and leave to cool — covering them will
make them sweat and make them easier to peel.

Remove the blackened skin from the capsicums by
gently rubbing it away with your fingertips — it should
come away easily. Cut away the stems and seeds
from inside the capsicums. The flesh is now ready
to eat or use.

shaved coconut

This may not be the traditional way of attacking a
coconut but it's the easiest way I know of. I have been
known to throw them out of second-storey windows,
but this can be dangerous to innocent passers-by!

1 coconut

Preheat the oven to 200°C (400°F/Gas 6) and put the
coconut on a shallow baking tray. Warm the coconut
in the oven for 5–10 minutes, or until the shell is starting
to crack. Remove from the oven and allow to cool.

Using a blunt knife, prise the shell of the cooled coconut
open — it should easily split apart. Remove the flesh
by wedging the knife between the flesh and the shell.
When the flesh has come away, you can shave it using
a vegetable peeler, or grate it with a cheese grater.

steamed coconut rice

400 g (14 oz/2 cups) white long-grain rice
750 ml (26 fl oz/3 cups) light coconut milk
1 pandan leaf, tied in a knot
1/2 teaspoon sea salt
1 teaspoon butter

Put the rice in a large bowl and cover with water. Stir several times, then drain away the water. Repeat this process several times to remove some of the starch from the rice.

Put the washed rice and all the remaining ingredients in a saucepan and bring to the boil. Reduce the heat to the lowest setting, cover the saucepan and cook for 30 minutes. Discard the pandan leaf before serving. Serves 6 as a side dish

steamed white rice

200 g (7 oz/1 cup) white long-grain rice
435 ml (15 1/4 oz/1 3/4 cups) water

Put the rice in a saucepan with a tight-fitting lid. Cover with the water and add a pinch of sea salt. Bring to the boil, then stir once to ensure the grains have not stuck to the base of the pan.

Cover the pan and turn the heat down to the lowest setting. Cook the rice for 15 minutes, then take the pan off the heat and allow the rice to sit for a further 10 minutes. Just before serving, fluff up the grains with a fork. Serves 2–4 as a side dish

sweet chilli sauce

5 garlic cloves, peeled
2 large red chillies, green stems removed
10 cm (4 inch) piece of lemon grass, trimmed
    and finely chopped
6 cm (2 1/2 inch) knob of ginger, peeled and
    roughly chopped
5 cm (2 inch) knob of galangal, peeled and
    roughly chopped
10 makrut (kaffir lime) leaves, cut into thin strips
1 handful coriander (cilantro) leaves
100 ml (3 1/2 fl oz) Chinese black vinegar
2 tablespoons fish sauce
2 tablespoons soy sauce
345 g (12 oz/1 1/2 cups) caster (superfine) sugar

Blend the garlic, chillies, lemon grass, ginger, galangal, lime leaves and coriander to a rough paste in a mini food processor. Mix the vinegar, fish sauce and soy sauce together in a small bowl.

Put the sugar in a saucepan with 4 tablespoons of water and stir over medium heat until the sugar has dissolved. Now turn the heat to high and cook for 4 minutes, or until the sugar is beginning to colour. Keeping a constant watch, continue boiling the sugar until it is almost burning and has a wonderful toffee smell.

Quickly add the spice paste, stir for 1 minute, then stir in the vinegar mixture. Cook for a further 2 minutes, then take the pan off the heat. Allow to cool, then pour into a clean glass jar. Cover and refrigerate until ready to use. The sauce will keep for several weeks in the refrigerator. Makes 330 ml (11 1/4 fl oz/1 1/3 cups)

sweet recipes

cardamom almond bread

3 egg whites
80 g (2³/4 oz/¹/3 cup) caster (superfine) sugar
85 g (3 oz/²/3 cup) plain (all-purpose) flour
zest of 2 oranges
90 g (3¹/4 oz/¹/2 cup) blanched almonds
¹/4 teaspoon ground cardamom

Preheat the oven to 180°C (350°F/Gas 4). Grease an 8 x 22 cm (3¹/4 x 8¹/2 inch) loaf (bar) tin and line it with baking paper. Whip the egg whites until they are stiff, then slowly whisk in the sugar. When the sugar has been fully incorporated and the whites are glossy, fold in the flour, orange zest, almonds and cardamom. Spoon the mixture into the prepared tin and bake for 40 minutes.

Cool the almond bread on a wire rack. When the loaf is cold, cut it into thin slices with a serrated knife and spread them out on a baking tray. Bake at 140°C (275°F/ Gas 1) for 15 minutes, or until the slices are crisp. Allow to cool completely on a wire rack before storing in an airtight container. Makes about 30 slices

pistachio biscotti

125 g (4¹/2 oz/1 cup) plain (all-purpose) flour
115 g (4 oz/¹/2 cup) caster (superfine) sugar
1 teaspoon baking powder
150 g (5¹/2 oz/1 cup) shelled pistachio nuts
2 teaspoons grated orange zest
2 eggs, beaten

Preheat the oven to 180°C (350°F/Gas 4). Mix the flour, sugar, baking powder, pistachios and orange zest together in a large bowl. Make a well in the centre and fold in the eggs to make a sticky dough.

Turn out onto a clean, floured surface. Divide the dough into two portions and roll each one into a log about 4 cm (1¹/2 inches) long. Put them on a baking tray lined with baking paper, leaving some space in between to allow for spreading. Bake for 30 minutes, then remove from the oven and allow to cool.

Reduce the oven temperature to 140°C (275°F/Gas 1). Using a very sharp bread knife, cut each loaf into thin slices about 5 mm (¹/4 inch) thick. Sit the biscuits on a baking tray and bake for 20 minutes, turning once during baking. Remove from the oven and cool on wire racks. Makes 30 to 40 biscuits

shortcrust tart case

200 g (7 oz/1²/3 cups) plain (all-purpose) flour
100 g (3¹/2 oz) chilled unsalted butter
2 tablespoons chilled water

Put the flour, butter and a pinch of salt in a food processor and process for 1 minute. Add the chilled water and process until the mixture comes together. Wrap the dough in plastic wrap and refrigerate for 30 minutes.

Grease a 25 cm (10 inch) tart tin or six 8 cm (3¹/4 inch) tartlet tins. Roll the pastry out as thinly as possible between two layers of plastic wrap, then use it to line the prepared tin or tins. Chill for a further 30 minutes.

Preheat the oven to 180°C (350°F/Gas 4). Using a fork, prick the pastry case/s over the base, line with crumpled baking paper and fill with rice or baking weights. Bake for 10–15 minutes, or until the pastry looks cooked and dry. Remove from the oven and allow to cool. Makes 1 large or 6 small tartlet cases

Note: If you are not using the tart case immediately, it will keep in the freezer for several weeks. There is no need to thaw before using — simply put it in the preheated oven direct from the freezer.

walnut bread

450 g (1 lb/3²/3 cups) plain (all-purpose) flour
1 heaped teaspoon bicarbonate of soda (baking soda)
1 heaped teaspoon cream of tartar
1 tablespoon sugar
1 teaspoon sea salt
500 ml (17 fl oz/2 cups) buttermilk
4 tablespoons finely chopped walnuts
2 tablespoons butter, melted

Preheat the oven to 200°C (400°F/Gas 6). Mix the flour, bicarbonate of soda, cream of tartar, sugar and sea salt together in a large bowl. Make a well in the centre and gradually add the buttermilk, combining to form a soft dough. Slowly fold the walnuts through.

Brush a 21 x 10 cm (8¹/4 x 4 inch) loaf (bar) tin with the melted butter. Put the dough into the greased tin and pour over any remaining butter. Bake for 30 minutes.

Reduce the oven temperature to 150°C (300°F/Gas 2) and bake for a further 30 minutes, or until a skewer inserted into the centre comes out clean. Turn the bread out onto a wire rack to cool. Makes 1 loaf

glossary

balsamic vinegar
Balsamic vinegar is a dark, aged vinegar made from grape juice. It is valued for its fragrant, sweetish taste. The production of authentic balsamic vinegar is carefully controlled. Bottles of the real thing are labelled 'Aceto Balsamico Tradizionale de Modena', while commercial varieties simply say 'Aceto Balsamico de Modena'.

betel leaf
This delicate green leaf, also known as *char plu*, is commonly eaten raw in Thai cuisine, where it is often used as a base or a wrapping for the small appetizers known as *miang*. The leaves are sold in bunches in Thai or Asian speciality shops.

black-eyed peas
Black-eyed peas (sometimes also called black-eyed beans) are small, cream-coloured kidney beans with a distinctive black spot.

black rice
This form of glutinous rice owes its colour to the layer of bran left intact on the grain which colours the rice as it cooks, resulting in a uniformly purplish-black rice. Predominantly used for sweet dishes in Thailand and the Philippines, it is available from Asian food stores.

black sesame seeds
Mainly used in Asian cooking, black sesame seeds add colour, crunch and a distinct nuttiness to whatever dish they garnish. They can be found in most Asian grocery stores. Purchase the seeds regularly, as they can become rancid with age. See also sesame seeds.

bocconcini cheese
These are small balls of fresh mozzarella, often sold sitting in their own whey. When fresh, they are soft and springy to the touch and have a milky taste. They are available from delicatessens.

broccolini
Broccolini is a cross between gai larn and broccoli, resulting in a green vegetable with long, thin stems and small florets. A more delicate version of broccoli, it is ideal for steaming, blanching and stir-frying.

buckwheat noodles
A speciality of northern Japan, buckwheat or soba noodles can be made entirely from buckwheat, but are often combined with a percentage of flour. These thin, highly nutritious noodles provide protein, calcium, iron and rutin.

burghul
Popular in the Middle East, burghul (bulgar) is the key ingredient in tabouleh and pilaff. You can buy these wheat kernels either whole or cracked into fine, medium or coarse grains. They are pre-steamed and pre-baked to minimize cooking time.

buttermilk
This cultured, low-fat dairy product is made from skim milk and milk powder and has a tart taste. It is often used in baking as a raising agent and can be found in the refrigerated section of supermarkets.

capers
Capers are the green buds from a Mediterranean shrub, preserved in brine or salt. Salted capers have a firmer texture and are often smaller than those preserved in brine. The salted capers have a better flavour, and the salt they are preserved in is a wonderfully flavoured alternative to sea salt for seasoning certain dishes.

cardamom
A dried seed pod native to India, cardamom is the third most expensive spice after saffron and vanilla. When crushed, the inner seeds give off a sweet, strong aroma. Cardamom is used whole or ground and can be found in the spice section of most supermarkets. Use sparingly, as it has quite a strong flavour.

casareccia
These short lengths of rolled and twisted Italian pasta are traditionally served with a meat sauce. This style of pasta is now commercially produced and is available in most large supermarkets.

chinese black vinegar
This rice vinegar is sharper than white rice vinegars and is traditionally used in stir-fries, soups and dipping sauces. The Chinese province of Chekiang has the reputation for producing the best black vinegars.

chinese five-spice
An aromatic mix of ground spices, Chinese five-spice is made from star anise, black pepper, fennel seeds, cassia and cloves. It can be rubbed into the skin of chicken or duck, or used sparingly to add an interesting flavour to pork or beef.

chinese salted black beans
These salted black beans can be found either vacuum-packed or sold in tins in Asian food stores. Their strong flavour can be used to bring a rich saltiness to stir-fries and sauces for beef dishes.

chocolate
Couverture is the best-quality chocolate for cooking. This bittersweet chocolate contains the highest percentage of cocoa butter.

It is available from gourmet stores and good delicatessens, but if you are unable to obtain chocolate of this standard, it is preferable to use a good-quality eating chocolate rather than a cheap cooking chocolate. Cooking chocolates, on the whole, do not have a good flavour and tend to result in an oily rather than a buttery texture.

cinnamon
Commonly sold in powdered form, cinnamon can also be bought in long 'quills' of bark, sometimes up to 1 metre (several feet) long.

coconut
The coconut is a common cooking ingredient in the Pacific, South-East Asia and India. The flesh is often grated or shredded and then dried. Shredding coconut produces small thin strips of dried coconut which are often used decoratively in desserts. Dessicated coconut is finely grated coconut which has been dried. It can be used in savoury as well as sweet dishes. See also shaved coconut (Basics).

coconut cream/milk
Coconut milk is available in tins in most supermarkets and is made from freshly grated coconut. Slightly thicker than coconut milk, coconut cream is also sold in tins alongside coconut milk. If you can't get hold of it, use the thick cream off the top of a couple of tins of coconut milk instead. Pour the milk into a jug and leave it to settle — the cream will separate out at the top.

couscous
Couscous is the favoured dish of North Africa. It is made from a flour-coated granular semolina which is traditionally steamed in a *couscousiere*. Nowadays, instant couscous is available in most large supermarkets.

crème fraîche
A naturally soured cream that is lighter than sour cream, crème fraîche is available at gourmet food stores and some large supermarkets. Sour cream can usually be used as a substitute.

daikon
Daikon, or *mooli*, is a large white radish. Its flavour varies from mild to surprisingly spicy, depending on the season and variety. Daikon contains an enzyme that aids digestion. It can be freshly grated or slow-cooked in broths, and is available from most large supermarkets or Asian grocery stores. Select firm and shiny vegetables with unscarred skins.

dashi granules
A common ingredient in Japanese cooking, dashi is a stock base made from dried kelp and flakes of dried bonito (a type of fish). Instant dashi can be bought from Asian food stores. Follow the manufacturer's instructions and simply add water to make an easy stock.

dried chinese egg vermicelli
These very thin noodles are made from wheat flour, water and egg. They are normally packaged in small neat bundles of dried yellow noodles.

dried limes
Traditionally used in Persian cuisine, dried limes are small, black and withered-looking and feel hard and almost hollow. They add an exquisite flavour to dishes and are sold by Middle Eastern grocers.

enoki mushrooms
These pale, delicate mushrooms have long, thin stalks and tiny caps. They are very fragile and need only a minimal cooking time. They are quite bland in flavour but have an interesting texture and appearance, so are ideal for blending with other mushrooms or for adding to Asian stir-fries for an exotic touch.

feta cheese
Feta is a firm, white cheese made from sheep's milk or goat's milk. The fresh cheese is salted and cut into blocks before being matured in its own whey. It must be kept in the whey or in oil during storage or it will deteriorate quickly. Bulgarian feta is not as sharply flavoured as the traditional Greek variety. Feta is available from delicatessens and most supermarkets.

fine semolina
Semolina is made of coarse granules of durum wheat. Fine semolina has smaller grains and is available from gourmet food stores.

fish sauce
This pungent, salty liquid made from fermented fish is widely used in South-East Asian cooking to add a salty, savoury flavour. Buy a small bottle and store it in the fridge.

french or red asian shallots
These small onions have a thin, papery skin and grow in bunches. They are also sometimes referred to as eschallots.

galangal
Although a member of the ginger family, galangal has a distinctly different flavour to ginger. Its fragrance is exquisitely perfumed, with a subtle hint of camphor. The root, although similar to ginger in appearance, is quite fibrous and tough, making it difficult to chop. Galangal is most commonly used in the cuisines of Malaysia and Indonesia and comes into its own in the soups of Thailand. It can be bought fresh, or sliced and preserved in brine in bottles from Asian grocery stores.

gelatine leaves
Leaf gelatine is available in sheets of varying sizes. Be careful to check the manufacturer's instructions regarding which ratio of liquid to gelatine sheet to use. If leaves are unavailable, use gelatine powder instead, making sure it is well dissolved in warm liquid during use. Once again, refer to the manufacturer's instructions.

goat's cheese
This is a soft, fresh cheese made from goat's milk. Goat's cheese has a slightly acidic but mild and creamy flavour.

hoisin sauce
A Chinese sauce made from a base of fermented soya beans. Hoisin has a distinctive salty, sweet flavour with a hint of garlic and five-spice.

horseradish

Large and white with a knobbly brown skin, horseradish is a root belonging to the mustard family. It is very pungent and has a spicy, hot flavour. It is usually freshly grated as a condiment for roast beef and smoked fish. When commercially produced, horseradish is often blended with cream to give it a smoother texture. Dollop on roast beef or smoked salmon.

indian lime pickle

Lime pickle is available from Indian grocery stores or large supermarkets. It is usually served as a side dish in Indian cooking.

japanese pickled ginger

Japanese pickled ginger is available from most large supermarkets. The thin slivers of young ginger root are pickled in sweet vinegar and turn a distinctive salmon-pink colour in the process. This soft pink colour is often exaggerated to a hot pink colour in commercially produced ginger, due to the addition of food colouring. The vinegar it is pickled in is terrific in sauces where a sweet, gingery bite is called for.

kecap manis

This is a thick, sweet-flavoured soy sauce used in Indonesian cooking.

lemon grass

These long, fragrant stems are very popular in Thai cuisine. The tough outer layers should be stripped off first, and the stem can then be used either finely chopped or whole in soups. Lemon grass will keep refrigerated for up to 2 weeks.

light olive oil

Light olive oil is a refined olive oil which is light in colour and flavour. It is ideal for cooking, or for recipes that would be overpowered by a more strongly flavoured oil.

makrut leaves

The glossy leaves of this South-East Asian tree (also called a kaffir lime) impart a wonderful citrusy flavour to food. Where possible, always use fresh, rather than dried, leaves.

mesclun

Mesclun is a green salad mix originating in Provence, France. It often features a selection of young, small leaves.

mirin

Mirin is a rice wine used in Japanese cooking. It adds sweetness to many sauces and dressings, and is used for marinating and glazing dishes. It is available from Asian grocery stores and most supermarkets.

miso paste

An important ingredient in Japanese cooking, miso paste is made from fermented soya beans and other flavourings such as wheat, rice or barley. It is used as a flavouring and a condiment. See also white miso.

mizuna

These tender young salad leaves have a pleasant, peppery flavour.

mozzarella cheese

Fresh mozzarella can be found in most delicatessens and is identified by its smooth, white appearance and ball-like shape. It is not to be confused with mass-produced mozzarella, which is mostly used as a pizza topping. Mozzarella is usually sold packed in whey.

mustard seeds

Mustard seeds have a sharp, hot flavour that is tempered by cooking. Both brown and yellow are available, although brown mustard seeds are more common.

natural vanilla extract

When using vanilla essence, always ensure it is made from real vanilla and is not labelled 'imitation' vanilla extract or essence. The flavours are quite different, with the imitation being almost acrid in its aftertaste. See also vanilla bean.

niçoise olives

Niçoise or Ligurian olives are small black olives that are commonly used in salads or scattered over prepared dishes. They are not suitable for stoning and making into pastes.

nori

Nori is an edible seaweed sold in paper-thin sheets. To concentrate the flavour, lightly roast the shiny side of the sheets over a low flame or in a hot oven for several minutes. Nori sheets are sold in large supermarkets and Asian grocery stores.

orange flower water

This perfumed distillation of bitter orange blossoms is used to flavour baked goods and drinks. It is readily available from large supermarkets and delicatessens.

oyster mushrooms

These beautifully shaped, delicately flavoured mushrooms are commonly white or a pale, greyish brown, but can also be pink or yellow. They are often also called abalone mushrooms. Their flavour is quite sharp when raw, making them suitable for creamy pasta or stir-fried dishes.

palm sugar

Palm sugar is obtained from the sap of various palm trees and is sold in hard cakes or cylinders and in plastic jars. If it is very hard it will need to be grated. It can be found in Asian grocery stores and large supermarkets. Soft brown sugar can be used instead.

pandan leaf

This fragrant leaf of a type of pandanus tree is widely used in South-East Asian cooking to flavour rice dishes and sweets. It is sold in Asian grocery stores.

papaya

This large tropical fruit can be red, orange or yellow. It contains an enzyme that stops gelatine setting, so avoid using it in jellies. It is sometimes called a pawpaw, but is really part of the custard apple family.

preserved lemon

These are whole lemons preserved in salt or brine, making their rind soft and pliable. Only the rind is used in cooking — the bitter, salty pulp should be scraped out and thrown away. Preserved lemons are available from delicatessens.

217

prosciutto

Prosciutto is lightly salted, air-dried ham. It is most commonly sold in paper-thin slices at delicatessens. Parma ham and San Daniele are both types of prosciutto.

puy lentils

Originally grown in the volcanic soils of the Puy region in France, these lentils are highly prized for their flavour and the fact that they hold their shape during cooking.

quinoa

A grain native to South America, quinoa is high in protein and very nourishing as it contains all eight essential amino acids. A wonderful base for salads and hearty sauces, quinoa is an ideal substitute for brown rice and has a similar nutty flavour. It is available from health food stores.

raw caster sugar

Also known as superfine sugar, this is a finer form of raw sugar. It brings a lovely brown tone to the food it is used to sweeten, and a slightly caramel flavour.

rice noodle sheets

These are simply flat sheets of fresh rice noodles, available from Asian grocery stores. The sheets can be cut into strips to make a rough noodle, or wrapped around cooked ingredients to make tasty little parcels.

rice wine vinegar

Made from fermented rice, this vinegar can be clear, red or black. If no colour is specified in a recipe, use the clear vinegar. The clear rice wine vinegar is sweeter and milder than the European vinegars or the darker and sharper-flavoured Chinese black vinegar.

rosewater

The distilled essence of rose petals, rosewater is used in small quantities to impart a perfumed flavour to pastries, fruit salads and puddings. It is available from delicatessens and large supermarkets.

saffron threads

The world's most expensive spice, saffron threads are the orange-red stigmas from a species of crocus plant, which are hand-picked, then dried — a very laborious process. Fortunately, saffron has a very strong flavour, so a very small amount goes a long way. Beware of inexpensive brands — cheap, 'real' saffron does not exist!

sashimi-grade salmon

Salmon sold for making sushi and sashimi is intended to be eaten raw, and so is usually the freshest fish at the markets. Buy a thick piece cut from the centre rather than the narrower tail end.

sea salt

Sea salt is a type of table and cooking salt obtained through a process of natural evaporation. Unlike common table and iodized salt, it contains no additives and so has a purer flavour. It is a little more expensive than regular salt, but its superior flavour easily justifies the extra cost. Look for it in the spice section of large supermarkets and speciality food stores, where it is sold in a range of grades, from fine grains through to flakes and coarse granules.

sesame oil

Sesame oil is available in two varieties. The darker, more pungent, type is made from roasted sesame seeds and comes from China, while the paler, non-roasted variety is Middle Eastern in origin.

sesame seeds

These tiny seeds, which grow in pods on several varieties of sesame plant, are reputed to be the world's oldest seasoning. White seeds are the most common, but there are also black, brown and red varieties. To enhance the flavour, lightly toast sesame seeds before using. Simply put them in a heavy-based frying pan over medium heat, lightly shaking the pan. When they start to turn golden brown, shake the pan a few more times to ensure they colour evenly, then quickly turn them out onto a plate. See also black sesame seeds.

shaoxing rice wine

This Chinese rice wine is used to add flavour to braised dishes and sauces. It takes its name from Shaoxing or Shao Hsing, a northern provincial town in China which has been producing rice wine for centuries. Shaoxing rice wine is similar to a fine sherry and is made from glutinous rice.

shiitake mushrooms

These Asian mushrooms have white gills and a brown cap. Meaty in texture, they keep their shape well when cooked. Dried shiitake are often sold as dried Chinese mushrooms.

sichuan peppercorns

These are made from the dried red berries of the prickly ash tree, which is native to Sichuan in China. The flavour is spicy-hot and leaves a numbing aftertaste, which can linger for some time. Dry-fry and crush the berries for the best flavour. Japanese sancho pepper is a close relative and may be used as a substitute.

smoked paprika

Paprika is commonly sold as a dried, rich red powder made from a member of the chilli family. It is sold in many grades, from delicate through to sweet and finally hot. Smoked paprika from Spain adds a distinct rich, smoky flavour to recipes and is well worth looking for if you enjoy introducing these flavours into your favourite dishes.

snow pea shoots

With their beautiful, swirling tendrils, these delicate young leaves and vine tips of the snow pea (mangetout) plant are highly prized in Asian cuisine. Add them raw to salads, or toss them into stir-fried dishes during the final minute of cooking.

somen noodles

These thin, wheat-based Japanese noodles are commonly sold dried and in bundles. They are available from Japanese speciality stores, large supermarkets and health food shops.

squid

You can often buy cleaned squid from fishmongers, but if you wish to clean squid yourself, here's how to do it. First remove the body from the head by gently pulling away the tentacles. Ensure the intestines have come away by running your finger around the interior of the tube, removing the plastic–like quill as you do so. Rinse the squid under running water, pulling away the semi-transparent skin. Next, remove the tentacles from the head by cutting through the flesh between the eyes and the tentacles. Feel around the centre of the tentacles for any tough membrane, and the small beak-like mouth. Remove and rinse under running water. Depending on your recipe, you can then cut the cleaned squid into rings using a sharp knife, or slice down one side of the squid, open it into a flat piece and score the softer inside surface with shallow crisscross incisions, then slice it into strips or pieces for cooking.

star anise

This is a pretty, star-shaped dried fruit containing small, oval, brown seeds. Star anise has a flavour similar to anise, but is more liquorice-like. It is commonly used whole because of its decorative shape.

sumac

Sumac is a peppery, sour spice made from dried and ground sumac berries. The fruit of a shrub found in the northern hemisphere, it is typically used in Middle Eastern cookery. Sumac is available from most large supermarkets and Middle Eastern speciality stores.

tahini

This is a thick, creamy paste made from ground white sesame seeds. It is used to give a strong nutty flavour to Middle Eastern salads or sauces. Tahini is sold in jars in health food stores and most supermarkets.

tamarind

Tamarind is the sour pulp of an Asian fruit. It is most commonly available compressed into cakes, or refined into tamarind purée, which is sold in jars. Tamarind purée is widely available in Asian food shops. To make tamarind water from compressed tamarind, put 100 g (3^{1}/2 oz) of tamarind into a bowl and cover with 500 ml (17 fl oz/2 cups) of boiling water. Allow to steep for 1 hour, stirring occasionally to break up the fibres, then strain.

tatsoi

Related to bok choy (pak choy), tatsoi is an Asian salad vegetable with small, flavoursome dark green leaves that can be tossed raw through salads, or added briefly to stir-fries.

thai basil

Thai basil is a distinctively flavoured herb with narrower and more deeply coloured leaves than the common basil.

tofu

This white curd is made from soya beans and is a wonderful source of protein. Although tofu is quite bland in taste, it takes on the flavour of the other ingredients it is cooked with. Tofu is usually sold in blocks in the refrigerated section of supermarkets and Asian grocery stores. It is available in several different forms — soft (silken), firm, sheets and even deep-fried. Refrigerate fresh tofu covered in water for up to five days, changing the water daily.

truss tomatoes

Truss tomatoes are simply those that are sold still on the vine.

vanilla bean

The long, slim, black vanilla bean has a wonderful caramel aroma that synthetic vanilla can never capture. Good-quality beans are soft and not too dry. Store unused vanilla pods in a full jar of caster (superfine) sugar, which will not only help to keep the vanilla fresh, but the aroma of the bean will quickly infuse the sugar, making it ideal for use in desserts and baking. See also natural vanilla extract.

vine leaves

The large, green leaves of the grapevine are available packed in tins, jars or plastic packs or in brine. They are used in Greek and Middle Eastern cuisine to wrap foods for cooking. Vine leaves sold in brine should be rinsed before use to remove some of the salty flavour. Fresh, young vine leaves should be simmered in water for 10 minutes, or until soft.

water chestnuts

The white, edible tuber of an aquatic plant, the water chestnut adds a delicate, crunchy texture to many South-East Asian dishes. Fresh water chestnuts can be found in Chinese food stores, and are also sold whole or sliced in tins.

white miso

White miso (which is actually a pale yellow colour) is a fermented paste of soya beans, salt and either rice or barley. It has a sweet, mellow taste and a relatively low salt content. White miso is available from Asian grocery stores and health food stores. See also miso paste.

white pepper

White pepper is produced by removing the outer husk of the black peppercorn. It has a little more 'bite' than black pepper, yet without the overriding flavour. It is more commonly used in white sauces on account of its colour, but it is also wonderful in rich or creamy dishes that you wish to balance with a little heat.

wild rocket

A smaller version of the large-leafed rocket (arugula), wild rocket has delicate leaves but a strong peppery flavour that is perfect in salads.

witlof

Also called chicory or Belgian endive, this salad leaf has a bitter flavour and a crisp, crunchy texture when raw. Witlof is available in both pale yellow and purple varieties.

index

221

This edition first published in Canada in 2006 by Whitecap Books, 351 Lynn Ave.,
North Vancouver, British Columbia, Canada, V7J 2C4.
www.whitecap.ca

First published by Murdoch Books Pty Limited in 2005.
www.murdochbooks.com.au

Chief executive: Juliet Rogers
Publisher: Kay Scarlett

Design concept and design: Marylouise Brammer
Design manager: Vivien Valk
Project manager: Zoë Harpham
Editor: Katri Hilden
Photographer: Mikkel Vang
Stylist: Christine Rudolph
Food preparation: Ross Dobson
Production: Monika Vidovic and Monika Paratore
Photographer's assistant: Andrew Wilson
Stylist's assistant: Nina Ross

ISBN 1 55285 739 5
ISBN 978 1 55285 739 7

Printed by C & C Offset Printing Co., Ltd. Printed in CHINA.

IMPORTANT: Those who might be at risk from the effects of salmonella poisoning (the elderly,
pregnant women, young children and those suffering from immune deficiency diseases) should
consult their doctor with any concerns about eating raw eggs.

CONVERSION GUIDE: You may find cooking times vary depending on the oven you are using. For
fan-forced ovens, as a general rule, set the oven temperature to 20°C (35°F) lower than indicated in the
recipe. We have used 20 ml (4 teaspoon) tablespoon measures. If you are using a 15 ml (3 teaspoon)
tablespoon, for most recipes the difference will not be noticeable. However, for recipes using baking
powder, gelatine, bicarbonate of soda (baking soda) or small amounts of cornflour (cornstarch), add
an extra teaspoon for each tablespoon specified.

The Publisher thanks 'Bambu', Bison Australia, Kris Coad, Phil Elson, Allan Fox, Market Import,
Step Back Antiques, Turtle Island, Vatulele Island Resort and Wonki ware for their assistance with the
photography for this book. Also, a huge thank you to Voyages and Heron Island for so generously
allowing our photography team to stay on the island and use it as a backdrop to the food.